BLESSED MODE

90 DAYS
TO LEVEL UP YOUR FAITH

KEL MITCHELL

THOMAS NELSON
Since 1798

Blessed Mode

© 2021 by Kel Mitchell

Published in Nashville, Tennessee, by Thomas Nelson. Thomas Nelson is a registered trademark of HarperCollins Christian Publishing, Inc.

The author is represented by United Talent Agency, LLC, a Delaware limited liability company, 888 Seventh Avenue, 7th Floor, New York, New York 10106.

Unless otherwise noted, Scripture quotations are taken from the Holy Bible, New International Version®, NIV®. Copyright © 1973, 1978, 1984, 2011 by Biblica, Inc.® Used by permission of Zondervan. All rights reserved worldwide. www.zondervan.com. The "NIV" and "New International Version" are trademarks registered in the United States Patent and Trademark Office by Biblica, Inc.® Scripture quotations marked ESV are taken from the ESV® Bible (The Holy Bible, English Standard Version®), copyright © 2001 by Crossway, a publishing ministry of Good News Publishers. Used by permission. All rights reserved. Scripture quotations marked KJV are taken from the King James Version. Public domain. Scripture quotations marked NKJV are taken from the New King James Version®. © 1982 by Thomas Nelson. Used by permission. All rights reserved. Scripture quotations marked NLT are taken from the Holy Bible, New Living Translation. Copyright © 1996, 2004, 2015 by Tyndale House Foundation. Used by permission of Tyndale House Ministries, Carol Stream, Illinois 60188. All rights reserved. Scripture quotations marked AMP are taken from the Amplified® Bible (AMP). Copyright © 2015 by The Lockman Foundation. Used by permission. www.lockman.org. Scripture quotations marked CEV are taken from the Contemporary English Version. Copyright © 1991, 1992, 1995 by American Bible Society. Used by permission. Scripture quotations marked MSG are taken from THE MESSAGE. Copyright © 1993, 2002, 2018 by Eugene H. Peterson. Used by permission of NavPress. All rights reserved. Represented by Tyndale House Publishers, Inc. Scripture quotations marked TLB are taken from The Living Bible. Copyright © 1971. Used by permission of Tyndale House Publishers, Inc., Carol Stream, Illinois 60188. All rights reserved.

Art direction: Tiffany Forrester

Interior design: Emily Ghattas

ISBN: 978-1-4002-2919-2 (audiobook)
ISBN: 978-1-4002-2920-8 (eBook)
ISBN: 978-1-4002-2918-5 (HC)

Printed in the United States

21 22 23 24 25 JOS 10 9 8 7 6 5 4 3 2 1

To my wife, Asia. You encouraged me to stay
consistent with motivating people on Instagram
with my #MrMitchellMorningMotivation posts,
which was the spark that ignited the flame of
the #GoGetThemBlessings mindset! Thank
you for the push, my love. Blessed mode!

CONTENTS

4

I'm Kel Mitchell. You might know me from the beloved sketch show for kids *All That* (a show I helped make iconic in the nineties and which I am currently producing the recent reboot on Nickelodeon), the spinoff sitcom *Kenan & Kel*, the film *Good Burger*, *Dancing with the Stars*, my time as host of CBS's *Best Friends FurEver*, and as a panelist on MTV's *Deliciousness*, the food-themed spinoff of MTV's *Ridiculousness*, as well as a number of other roles.

But my favorite role might surprise you. I followed the path God had been preparing for me: I became a youth pastor.

Not many pastors stay in the entertainment business while still pastoring (I know of one: Mr. Fred Rogers), but I've been so incredibly blessed and so inspired by God's love that I had to give back. God has changed my life in profound ways. For more than eight years, I have been involved in Helps Ministry at my church, Spirit Food Christian Center, and three years ago, Pastor Garry D. Zeigler saw God's call on my life to teach youth. So when I'm not acting, producing, or working on the honey-do list for my beautiful wife, Asia, and daddy duties for my awesome children, I'm at Spirit Food Christian Center and out in my community, speaking to youth across the country, encouraging them to trust in the Lord and follow their dreams, to inspire others, and to fulfill the life God has for them.

Now I want to bring some of the lessons I've learned into a devotional full of inspiration for those who long to walk in God's grace and wake up every day expecting to receive blessings because of their obedience in trusting the Lord with all their heart.

What's it about? This devotional focuses on one of my favorite subjects: God's blessings, the gifts we receive when we put total trust and faith in Him. Each entry focuses on how to notice blessings, receive blessings, share blessings, and create blessings for others.

Who is it for? This devotional is for anyone! It's for anyone looking to strengthen their relationship with God, but it's especially for people who feel stuck or are seeking renewed inspiration. We all stumble on this journey of life. Sometimes we create emotional walls and blocks that are so high and wide that we can't see our way out. These walls can begin to feel like actual physical walls, blocking us from a blessed future.

But I want to show you that you can break through these emotional walls by changing your perspective! When we focus on the One who can show us the way out of a world of setbacks, we'll see a world full of blessings.

The Lord gives us hope. He said it to us loud and clear in the Bible:

"'For I know the plans and thoughts that I have for you,' says the Lord, 'plans for peace and well-being and not for disaster, to give you a future and a hope'" (Jeremiah 29:11 AMP).

When you focus on the One who can give you a blessed future, He will give you concrete plans to get there.

Why did I write it? To encourage you! Too often, people make the mistake of trying to break through their emotional walls on their own, thinking they can solve life's problems alone. I did the same thing, and for years my negative thoughts controlled my life. I would make bad decisions and feel guilty every time I repeated a mistake, telling myself over and over that if I hadn't messed up, I'd be experiencing God's blessings by now.

I was so consumed by past mistakes that I had constant anxiety about the future. It got so bad that I felt for a while like I was slowly vanishing. The Enemy would have loved for me to give up and turn off the light God had put inside me. But I chose to seek the Light!

Everything changed for me when I decided to be obedient and have faith in God's Word and in His promise to give me a bright future and a continual hope. So I began working to release my negative mindset and pursue real change in my life. I knew this wouldn't be easy, but when I put my full faith in God, I began seeing ways to go after the blessings on the other side of that emotional wall. I decided to create a joyful future! I picked up the sledgehammer of faith and slammed it against that wall of regret and negativity.

Now, did the wall fall right away? No, of course not. But the first hit created a small crack, and a sliver of light shined through. This light ignited a healing in my life, and I felt like God was saying to me, "I'm still here. I love you, and I've got some plans for you. Now let's go get them blessings."

A blessed exit exists inside every emotional wall. God *never* leaves us alone! If you trust Him and listen closely, you will hear Him knocking: "Behold, I stand at the door and knock. If anyone hears my voice and opens the door, I will come in to him and eat with him, and he with me" (Revelation 3:20 ESV). You only have to let Him in!

As you read through the pages of *Blessed Mode*, you'll be

widening that crack of light a little bit, day by day, so you can discover God's blessings on you. Focus on the light in that small crack, and let it heal and restore you. All you need is a little bit of faith to start receiving God's blessings, and soon you will believe, like me, that nothing is impossible.

Let this book be a blessing to you.

"For if you had faith even as small as a tiny mustard seed, you could say to this mountain, 'Move!' and it would go far away. Nothing would be impossible."

MATTHEW 17:20 TLB

INTRODUCTION

There's a *lot* of negativity out there in the world. If you spend too much time focusing on the news, people's negative attitudes, the hardships we all endure, and more, you could really get sucked into a spiral of negativity. Stress and anxiety are at all-time highs, turning many of us into chronic worriers who dwell on the difficulties and troubles of this world instead of focusing on the positive.

You might be reading this and thinking to yourself, *What is the positive in my life?* Perhaps you're trying to find a light in all the darkness from past mistakes, trauma, or struggle. It sucks knowing you can't control situations. I know because I've been there. But here's some good news: we *can* control our thoughts, reactions, behavior, and what we believe.

Life is about choices, and you can choose to keep your joy, happiness, and peace by *planning* to keep your joy, happiness, and peace—regardless of your circumstances. If you plan to respond in a peaceful manner to a rude person or keep your joy in a bad situation, that's where you gain some freedom. By controlling your responses to people and to the circumstances of life, you have the power to create blessed opportunities with God!

When you wake up each day, you probably already know many of the things that might distract you or bring you down, the things that might tempt you or trip you up. So why not go to God at the start of the day and create a strategy together? Ask Him to help you with the difficulties that might come, both those you know about and those you're not yet aware of. Get into a state of mind—or a mode—that makes you a divine reflection of God's power in every circumstance.

We have the ability to endure whatever comes our way when we make sure God is present in our lives and when we stay connected to Him, listening for His lovingkindness and promises. When we stay in this close relationship with God, we enter something I call *blessed mode*.

What is blessed mode? Well, I like to think of it like playing a video game. You start out with a set number of lives or points or coins. And then you work your way through obstacles and challenges, you fight battles and monsters, you slay dragons . . . and you gain new abilities and skills along the way. You start to level up. And then level up again. People will think you have some type of cheat codes!

Cheat codes are created by video game developers to help game testers skip levels, easily find items, and heal their character so they can efficiently test the game. They can be used to unlock special features for players by typing in the code that only the developer knows. Some games call this "God Mode"—because you know what the creator knows. If you apply this concept to "blessed mode," it means you are able keep advancing in life even when things look impossible—because God is with you.

Here's the best news about blessed mode: all God requires of us is to believe and to call on Him. When you're in blessed mode, you can be a reflection of God's greatness *at all times*! This book offers simple daily reminders of who God designed you to be. You are beautifully and wonderfully made and, like a video game avatar, capable of being charged up by God's power, making the impossible

possible in your life. Sometimes we can feel drained—because life can be hard. But this book is designed to *power you up*, to inspire you and build up your spirit each morning to conquer the day with righteous skills, faith, and the determination to keep your joy!

When you live in a state of blessed mode, people will wonder how you keep leveling up in life, and you will have the opportunity to show them that it's all God and His Holy Spirit. It may look to the world like you have a cheat code, but it's all God's favor and power bringing you wisdom, mercy, victory, and blessing. "Blessed be the Lord, who daily loads us with benefits, the God of our salvation!" (Psalm 68:19 NKJV).

Blessed Mode also includes the foundation for a spiritual game plan to combat negativity and reach for God's blessings. Each entry follows the same format so you can really get into a routine.

- A Bible verse. Each entry begins with one of my favorite scriptures, specific verses that keep me in blessed mode no matter what's happening around me.
- #BlessedMode. Next, I'll share stories and lessons from my own faith experiences with relatable insight and advice that I hope will be helpful on your journey.
- #LevelUpYourFaith. Then, I'll invite you to pray. Prayer doesn't have to be fancy or use big words. I think the simplest prayers are the most heartfelt. And prayer connects you to God and has the power to really change lives and circumstances, so let's level up in prayer!
- #GoGetThemBlessings. Finally, I'll ask you to put your faith in action and apply these principles to your own life with a fun and simple activity that will help you grow spiritually.

My dream is to create a community of people all over the world who love God and want to share His power with others. As we read through this ninety-day devotional together, you can share what is connecting with you most by using the above hashtags on social media. Let's blow up the internet with God's power and blessing as we share all about the love and grace we receive through His Son, Jesus Christ. There are so many ways to engage with this book and with others; I know you'll find something that helps get you into your own blessed mode and inspires you to spread the word.

It's time to make God part of your everyday life and to receive all the blessings He has for you! Press the start button in 3 . . . 2 . . . 1 . . . *blessed mode*!

"You are the light of the world—like a city on
a hilltop that cannot be hidden."
MATTHEW 5:14 NLT

Have you ever seen or caught lightning bugs? When I was a kid,
I loved to catch fireflies and watch them light up my hands or a
jar for a few minutes. Lightning bugs light up the night sky all on
their own and communicate with this bioluminescence, flashing
in a particular pattern as they fly around. And each of the more
than two thousand species of lightning bugs has *its own* special
flash pattern so they don't attract different species. Isn't creation
amazing?

My wife, Asia, and I have a similar flash pattern. Something
about each of us communicated to the other's soul that God was
bringing us together. In the beginning stages of our relationship,
I couldn't explain this feeling. God helped me understand as I
remembered back to being a kid, lying in the tall grass, the sun
warming me, not a worry in the world. That peaceful memory was
God showing me, "Yeah, you've been through a lot, but I never
stopped loving you, and I have someone for you that I planned
before you were born." Asia came to me, God's gift, when He felt
I was spiritually ready.

When I proposed to Asia, I had turned off the electricity
to the house ahead of time. She walked in first after our date
and began flipping every light switch. "What's going on with the
lights?" she said as she went from room to room.

"I found the light!" I yelled from another room.

As she walked in, I opened a ring box with a small light inside that illuminated the engagement ring. Then I asked her to marry me (and she said yes!). It felt like our love lit up the entire house.

Maybe you've experienced something similar with a friend, family member, or spouse. Your lights attract the other person and then light adds to light. Your two lights combine to make one even *brighter* light. It's the same way with God. He is the Light of the World, and when we are close to him, our light is *His* light, shining for the world to see. When you turn on the light of God in your mind, body, and spirit, people with the same light will be drawn to you. Your relationships, career, and other areas of life will shine brighter too. And you'll begin to clearly see the path God wants you to take. Let's light it up for God!

#LevelUpYourFaith

Thank You, God, for shining Your light on me and for helping me to see the wonderful gifts You've given me. My heart is lit up for You, and I want others to see that light! Help me continue to walk in the light of Your Word. In Jesus' name I pray, amen.

#GoGetThemBlessings

Grab a candle and a Bible and turn to Matthew 5:14–16. Set the open Bible on a table, and safely light the candle and turn off the lights. As your eyes adjust, imagine God shining a calming light over you as you reflect on His words. Consider all the ways He is blessing you and how you can shine your light for the world to see.

2

ANCHORED AND SECURE

I like to hang paintings and art throughout our home. But some of the frames are so heavy. If I were to just hammer a nail into the wall and fling the artwork up there, I'd run the risk of the nail not holding and the art crashing to the ground (that's not exactly the kind of handyman I'm tryna be).

To keep our art and our home safe, I install wall anchors. Sometimes I use a plastic or metal anchor that acts as a grippy sleeve around the screw or nail, but for heavy-duty jobs, I hammer a nail directly into a stud—the wood frame behind the drywall. The studs—the framing of a house—are attached to the foundation. And those two things are what make a house secure and able to withstand storms and time—and to hold the heaviest of art. And you *know* when you've located a stud as soon as you begin to hammer or drill. The nail or screw will sort of bite down in a different way than with drywall. There's no mistaking it. You've hit something secure.

In Scripture, all these things represent God and our faith:

- Anchor: "We have this hope as an *anchor* for the soul, firm and secure" (Hebrews 6:19).
- Foundation: "But God's firm *foundation* stands" (2 Timothy 2:19 ESV).
- Firm: "I am present with you in spirit and delight to see how disciplined you are and how *firm* your faith in Christ is" (Colossians 2:5).

- Secure: "And you will feel *secure*, because there is hope; you will look around and take your rest in security" (Job 11:18 ESV).

When we are battered by life, we have to push in closer to the God we cannot see, much like those wall studs behind the drywall. We lean in and trust His Word, having faith that He will remain with us, keeping us firm and secure.

#LevelUpYourFaith

My hope is made strong because of You, Lord. Your love never fails. You hold me close and secure in Your arms, and I trust in You and Your holy Word. Thank You, Lord! In Jesus' name I pray, amen.

#GoGetThemBlessings

Get on the floor in a plank position. Hold it as long as possible. Your arms will start to shake, but only drop when you absolutely must! And be reminded that God always holds steady. When we are weak, He is strong. And we can grow in Him with steady relationship. As we build our faith, the foundation gets stronger, much like if you keep planking. As you get stronger each day, think about how God is strengthening your faith as well.

SUPER LIKE GLUE

I am convinced that nothing can ever separate us from [Christ's] love. Death can't, and life can't. The angels won't, and all the powers of hell itself cannot keep God's love away.
ROMANS 8:38 TLB

#BlessedMode

You ever notice how the word *super* can change the way you think about something? Like if I asked about your weekend and you said it was fun, I'd think, *Oh, okay. He had a good weekend. Cool.* But if you answered and said it was *super* fun, well, I'd want more information! Now we're talkin'! Tell me what happened, what made this weekend so super.

We have bikes and phone chargers, but then we also have superbikes and superchargers. Superman, Superwoman. Super smart and super dumb (and you know super dumb is way different than just dumb, LOL). Whether the word *super* is added to a negative or positive word, it completely changes the way we think about that word.

I have a little story about one of these "super" words: *Super Glue.* When I was young, I was intrigued by a Super Glue commercial and wanted to try it so badly. I secretly put some Super Glue on my friend's chair in class. I watched and waited as he sat down. It worked! He couldn't get back up because his pants were glued to the chair! The janitor had to cut off the seat and cut the fabric on my friend's pants so he could wriggle free. Nothing could separate that glue from *his* seat. (Oh, and do not—I repeat, do not—try this prank. It will result in you getting detention or grounded. I got both.)

Now you know why I'll never forget the power of Super Glue!

That wasn't just glue. It was *super* glue—a whole other level of stuck. Remembering that story got me thinking about this idea in a supernatural way because that's how it is with God too. We can't see Him, but we can know that He is with us, stuck to us like Super Glue. And nothing can break that bond—not people, life circumstances, nothing!

I will stick with You, Lord, because You always stick with me—a divine connection that leads to supernatural blessings. Your love is all-powerful. I won't worry about tomorrow because You keep me close and protected, and I thank You deeply for that. In Jesus' name I pray, amen.

Go to the grocery store and buy some popsicles. Then I want you to do something crazy: eat them, LOL. (If you're limiting junk food, just buy a pack of popsicle sticks.) Take the bare popsicles sticks, and superglue printed photos of yourself, your family, and your friends. Put these fun reminders in an important place and pray over each one, asking God to "stick" close to each person and to you.

Consider it pure joy, my brothers and sisters, whenever
you face trials of many kinds, because you know that
the testing of your faith produces perseverance.
JAMES 1:2–3

#BlessedMode

The year 2020 shocked us all, didn't it? But it did not break us! I learned about myself and had some open and loving conversations with people (and also some hard conversations). It was a year of much insight and experience, secrets revealed, Enemy attacks, spiritual breakthroughs, court cases, and answered prayers. I worked on two new television series, addressed my flaws, learned lessons, received blessings, got advice, and gave advice. My youngest son, Honor, was born. The relationship between my wife and I got even stronger as our communication and understanding grew, which led to our love growing stronger. I even wrote this book *during a pandemic* (never thought I'd type those words).

The year 2020 revealed a ton of things, and since the whole world experienced it together, I felt it was only right to talk about it. A week before Christmas 2020, I did an interview with *The Christian Post*. The reporter asked how the pandemic had affected me and if I could explain finding joy and faith in the midst.

Like everybody, my first reaction was shock. I thought this would be over in a week or two. But when it wasn't and everything started closing up, that's when I was like, *Okay, this is really real. This is a time to turn to God. And it's a time to slow down and focus on important things.*

We moved church gatherings onto social media, where young people conveniently already spend a lot of time. And even there,

God continued to do amazing things. Teens from different cities and around the world started to tune in.

Wow, I thought. *If this pandemic hadn't happened, these messages might not have reached this kid!* Sometimes a teen would log on to say, "Hey, I'm a fan of Kel Mitchell, but I also want to see this God he speaks so highly of." And then something would tug at them, maybe the sermon or a call to give their life to Christ. That's what this is all about!

Mostly, I was able to shift my mindset during this season, to see God at work and to be grateful amid chaos. I want that for you too, to focus on improving the condition of your mind during troubled times, to seek out faith, and to find joy in every moment.

#LevelUpYourFaith

I consider it all joy, Lord, because I know You work everything for good! Thank You for giving me peace and understanding and for revealing what I need to work on, showing more love to myself and others. I am so very grateful. In Jesus' name I pray, amen.

#GoGetThemBlessings

Remember, life is a gift! I like the acronym GIFT: God Is Forever There. He's there in my trouble, in my peace, in my flaws, in my triumphs, in my blessings. You can turn to Him at any time for guidance and help. You are so loved. Now, go get them blessings.

DON'T STOP BELIEVING

#BlessedMode

This is your daily pep talk, and I'm gonna keep this one super simple because we humans are very busy and have a tendency to forget. Ready?

Don't stop believing!

Trust in your faith. Remember when those things that you believed actually came true? Like when your friend was healed or that relationship was restored? *Believe.*

Remember how you felt when you saw faith manifested in your life and truth became a reality? *Believe.*

Remember how the blessing came upon you and you felt so much joy in your heart because you received such a special gift? *Believe.*

God has already done so much, and *He will not stop.* I will yell that truth from the mountaintops. So keep believing until you see it happen.

Today I am reminding you to never give up and never stop believing. Remember those times, remind yourself of them regularly, because God will do it again. All things are possible to those who believe in Him and in His power and might.

I love this verse: "I also pray that you will understand the incredible greatness of God's power for us who believe him. This is the same mighty power that raised Christ from the dead and seated him in the place of honor at God's right hand in the heavenly realms" (Ephesians 1:19–20). God *raised Christ from the dead*! Talk about powerful. Won't He do everything and more in your life?

#LevelUpYourFaith

God, I remember all You have done for me. I will not doubt Your power to keep doing amazing works in my life. I will not lose my faith in You or stop believing. In Jesus' name I pray, amen.

#GoGetThemBlessings

Search online for the song "I Believe" by the group Sounds of Blackness. Listen to the uplifting lyrics about believing in the power of God working in you. All things are possible!

Blessed is the one whom God corrects, so do not despise the discipline of the Almighty.
JOB 5:17

DIVINE CORRECTION

There's nothing like telling someone your plan . . . and then after a while they see you not following it anymore. Then, when they remind you of the plan you were so proud of, you get defensive! At least that's what I used to do.

I knew the person holding me accountable was doing what I'd asked. But when they'd see me falling away from the plan, I'd get so frustrated. "I know I fell off! I know I didn't stick with it!" My anger wasn't really with the accountability friend; it was with myself. I could see the pattern of my choices and actions veering from the plan. And I could see potential failure fast approaching. But I didn't want to receive that reality check! Because in the moment, the truth hurt. But the truth is the only thing that keeps us on track toward spiritual growth and maturity.

My accountability partner sometimes says to me, in a loving way, "What happened to your dedication?" That can feel like a low blow at first, but when I change my perspective, I realize that God will use whoever is in my path to get me spiritually back on course. People who hold us accountable are being used by the Lord to remind us, "Get up! Life isn't over! You can get on track!" So there's no need to react with anger when a trusted adviser calls you out. When I know I've been distracted from God's plan, I'm grateful that He loves me so much that He'll use His children to help me refocus on the ideas and plans He gave me because I am also His child.

Remember, God loves His children, and He sometimes shows His love by correcting us. When that happens, the reaction should never be anger or guilt. Try for gratefulness and react by listening instead. It took me some time to understand God's discipline, but I am so happy that I get it clearly now—and that is all because of God.

#LevelUpYourFaith

Lord, I won't get angry when You correct me. I consider it an honor to be so loved by you that You pull me by the coattails when I'm going the wrong way and get me on the right path. I open my ears to Your wisdom and guidance. I will listen with my whole heart. In Jesus' name I pray, amen.

#GoGetThemBlessings

An easy way to help create personal accountability is to set a few reminders on your phone for small tasks throughout the day that work on your wellness and spirit. Drink some water, do five minutes of breathing exercises, meditate on Scripture, take a walk. These are just some examples. Do what feels healthy to you.

Oh, that you would bless me and expand my territory! Please be with me in all that I do, and keep me from all trouble and pain!" And God granted him his request.
1 CHRONICLES 4:10 NLT

#BlessedMode

Everyone walks differently. We probably pick up our specific gaits by watching others. Babies certainly do this. They watch their older siblings or parents, and in their little baby minds, they're probably thinking, *One day,* I'm *gonna walk around this house and get my own bottle out of the fridge.* (Kudos if you read that in your best baby voice, LOL.) Then they start to pull themselves up on furniture and practice walking with assistance. And before you know it, their cute, wobbly baby steps turn into unassisted walking. They still might fall at times, but babies learn how to get back up and try again.

My youngest daughter, Wisdom, is a toddler, and it's awesome to see her discovering new things. When she was a year old, she would point at the front door and yell, "Outside!" That girl loves new places and adventures. When we took her to a new place, she'd baby-walk around with so much excitement, like, "I can *really* play here in this new place?" We knew she was safe, so we'd say, "Yes, my child." Then she'd give us a big hug and say, "Aww," which meant "thank you" in her little vocabulary. She was saying, "Thank you so much for bringing me here, for letting me walk around this new place that I never knew existed. This is awesome!"

God says "Yes, My child" to us too when He allows us to walk in new places. "You have practiced My Word and been obedient. Here is this new territory." A lot of the time, we go, "Really, God?!" and run around in our new blessing, thanking Him along the way. But sometimes in this new, blessed territory, we have to adjust. New obstacles, new experiences, people we've never interacted with. . . . It can feel overwhelming. But God is with you! Even in new, unfamiliar places.

As Christians, we will continue to step into new territory as we obey His Word and grow in our faith. And we can trust that God will be faithful to teach us as we learn to walk in each new territory and beyond.

#LevelUpYourFaith

Lord, I will trust the process. You know what is best for me! I will not complain, because what You have for me is far better than what I could imagine for myself. When I declare Your Word, You anoint my steps. Thank You, Lord, for Your grace! In Jesus' name I pray, amen.

#GoGetThemBlessings

Go outside and take a walk. As you walk, think about all the things the Lord has brought you through. Thank Him! As you look up at the sky, really acknowledge how big the world is. And still, He gives you the desires of your heart and takes you to places you've never been before. Praise Him for showing up and giving you an abundance of blessings!

8

ALL THAT GOD

"Think about all that you are instead of all that you are not."

I read this quote the other day, and it really spoke to me. It's so easy to focus on the negative, isn't it? I thought it was cool that this quote had the phrase "all that" in it. That's the name of the Nickelodeon sketch comedy show for kids that kicked off my television career.

But what does the name of the show mean? Where did we get it from? Back in the nineties, before the television show came out, people used the phrase "all that" in sentences like, "He's all that and a bag of chips!" or "He think he's all that," or "She think she's all that." Online definitions say things like, "Superior, as good as it gets, top of the top, too cool, has it all together, the best." And that's what our show was! Top of the top, too cool, as good as it gets!

Let's read the first quote a little more closely: "Think about all that you are instead of all that you are not." One phrase that really sticks out to me is "think about." Life really is how we perceive it, how we think about it. What do you believe? How do you view what happens to you or new circumstances or challenges? You have a *choice* to have a positive state of mind or a negative state of mind, a hopeful mind or a doubtful mind. The choice is really up to you. It may seem simplistic, but I believe it's true: change your thinking; change your life!

The beautiful thing about changing your mind, about *choosing* to change the way you perceive things, is that you can start anytime. It's never too late! "All that you are"? You have been created in God's image, so "all that you are" should be all of God. What more could we possibly want or hope for?

I sometimes like to use the phrase "all God" instead of "all that." If "all that" means superior in all things, "all God" is more than we can ask or imagine—*more than* superior. And it means we are able to do *all things* we put our minds to because of *all God* in us!

We are *all that* because of *all God* has done for us. So let's praise Him!

Lord, You are Alpha and Omega, the beginning and the end. You are all that and then some. And I can do all things because of You! I worship Your holy name. You give me strength to endure. All that I am and will be is because of Your protection and guidance. I give You praise! In Jesus' name I pray, amen.

#GoGetThemBlessings

Today, add "all God" to all aspects of your life. And I do mean *all*—walking the dog, running errands, working, studying, exercising. Whatever it is you do today, ask Him to be with you, to be in you, to assist and guide you. You will be surprised at the extra power you will have to be "all that" in God's power.

SPIRITUAL TRAINING

Every part of Scripture is God-breathed and useful one way or another—showing us truth, exposing our rebellion, correcting our mistakes, training us to live God's way. Through the Word we are put together and shaped up for the tasks God has for us.
2 TIMOTHY 3:16–17 MSG

#BlessedMode

I really like to work out. A while back, though, I was really struggling through my workout routines because of pain in my shoulder and neck and headaches. The pain was so severe that I finally decided to visit a chiropractor. After checking me over, she told me that one of my shoulders was more muscular than the other and that the other shoulder was pulling away to try to compensate for the imbalance. That was causing my issues.

She readjusted my shoulder so it wasn't pulling, corrected the proper joint function, and then said, "Make sure you are balanced and aligned properly when you're working out so this doesn't happen again. Listen to your body and correct when needed." That imbalance would keep leading to pain if I didn't actively work toward alignment.

Her words got me thinking. Life is a lot like a workout, isn't it? Much like how our muscles are put under pressure during exercise, the pressure of life affects our minds, our spirits, and more. That's not a bad thing. We grow and get stronger and more resilient with each rep. But we mustn't respond the way my shoulder was responding—by pulling away or compensating in a way that only creates more pain. Responding negatively to the pressures of life ultimately only adds anxiety, anger, and fear, which can cause us to lose our balance and move away from what God has planned for us.

God designed us to correct and to readjust as we encounter challenging situations. Today's verse reminds us that He has given us the tools we need—He's here to train and correct and to help us adjust no matter what happens. As long as we keep our faith and train our focus on Him—responding with love, praying, and meditating on His Word—we can stay in perfect alignment with His divine plan to prosper us and give us a delightful future.

#LevelUpYourFaith

Lord, I will continue to let You instruct me in every way. I will connect with You first before making any decisions. Please correct and adjust me mentally and spiritually and give me divine strength, endurance, and consistency to do Your will. You are my divine trainer, and I am ready to carry out Your purpose for me! In Jesus' name I pray, amen.

#GoGetThemBlessings

Exercise challenges are super popular on social media. Let's do our own! Since God is your spiritual trainer, let's try a fun challenge. At the start of every new hour today, take sixty seconds to thank God for all He has done and will do in your life. Set an alarm on your phone to remind you. As you wrap up this "workout" challenge before bed, take a moment to examine how this affected your day. You may discover that you want to continue this challenge with an accountability partner or friend.

Don't be angry or furious. Anger can lead to sin.
PSALM 37:8 CEV

UNBOTHERED

#BlessedMode

Being out of control is not fun. Even *feeling* out of control stinks! Have you ever seen the hashtag #unbothered on social media? It's so empowering to see people choose not to get riled up about a situation that normally might make them snap.

- Not allowing toxic people to distract you from your purpose. #unbothered
- Meditating and praying about issues instead of arguing. #unbothered
- Letting go of people pleasing and just being yourself. #unbothered
- Not taking people's opinions about you personally. #unbothered

When you're #unbothered, you choose not to trouble yourself with negativity that will stress you out or cause you to be reactive. It doesn't mean you don't care; it just means you won't allow negativity to disrupt your space, and you won't take part in toxic behavior. Rather, you focus on the positive. You aren't reactionary.

I used to be the opposite of #unbothered. I would freak out about stuff. And it was *not* fun. My heart would pound like crazy. I'd start to shake and would blurt out stupid, reactionary things, hurting people's feelings and disappointing myself in the process. Then I'd have to make a series of apologies for losing my cool. These outbursts would hurt people and harm my relationships.

It took me a while to figure this out, but I learned that when

I'm extremely stressed, when things don't go according to plan, that's when I'm likely to snap. I recognize that now. When I am faced with a stressful situation, I stop, loosen up, breathe deeply, and talk to God about it until I find peace.

When was the last time you felt this way? Stressed, angry, ready to snap, maybe even out of control? What might have happened if you had stopped everything and asked the Holy Spirit to guide your words? If your experience is anything like mine, everyone would have avoided pain. So many things can happen when we're reactionary—grudges, guilt, revenge, added anxiety and anger, and more. God doesn't want that for you. And He truly is your help when things feel out of control.

#LevelUpYourFaith

Lord, take my anxiety and my worries today. I will bring my concerns to You, Lord, and I will let them go. I want to spread kindness instead of negativity! Help me to remain peaceful today no matter what happens. In Jesus' name I pray, amen.

#GoGetThemBlessings

If a person or situation has been stressing you out, make a plan to stay unbothered. One great way to do this is by breathing intentionally while you pray. Breathe deeply and release your anger or stress as you pray these words: *Holy Spirit, guide my words with [person's name or situation]. You, Lord, are my help.* Breathe in and out as you repeat this prayer. When you breathe out, imagine exhaling the stress from your life.

HITTING THE TARGET

You intended to harm me, but God intended it for good to accomplish what is now being done, the saving of many lives.
GENESIS 50:20

#BlessedMode

The story of Joseph in the Bible (where today's verse is from) is straight up crazy. His brothers didn't like that he was their father's favorite, so they put him in a pit and then sold him into slavery. Talk about sibling rivalry! But the outcome for Joseph and his family didn't turn out at all like his brothers had predicted.

When the Enemy tries to destroy us, like he did with Joseph, we have options: we can sink into the pit, or we can grow stronger in our faith. Under this pressure, we often actually grow *faster*. And when we're released from the situation, we're able to come back stronger than ever.

I think it's a lot like archery. A bow and arrow doesn't work unless the string is pulled back taut. When the string is released, the arrow slices through the air, quick and with precision. In life, we're pulled back like that string a lot, holding challenges with tension, holding burdens that cause stress and keep that bow in our lives pulled back *tight*. In the middle of this pullback, we must pray, maintain our discipline, and be willing to sacrifice.

This all sounds like a lot of work, huh? I have some good news. Because of our faith, God is in that tension with us. And when we are released, He guides our arrow as we slice through the air to hit His will and blessings for our lives.

Unlike an archer, we can't always see the target we're aiming for. We have to rely on our faith—a faith that grows in godly focus and wisdom through praying, reading God's Word, listening for

His voice, and surrounding ourselves with His people. If we're doing that, we don't need to worry about the outcome. God is working; He knows the outcome. And that's how we hit the target every time.

So what happened with Joseph? After all that he endured because of his brothers' actions, Joseph remained faithful to God (you can read his whole story in Genesis 37–47), and when these same brothers were staring down death, *Joseph saved them*. Talk about hitting a target, especially one he never could have expected.

Keep going! Even amid struggles and attacks, God is with you, and ready to guide you to His target for you.

#LevelUpYourFaith

Sign me up, Lord! I am working with Your army. The battle is already won. I will not fear; I will trust! In Jesus' name I pray, amen.

#GoGetThemBlessings

Are you experiencing a place of hardship right now, pulled back taut like the string on a bow? Draw a bull's-eye with three rings and write down what you're dealing with in the outer ring. Write God's name in the ring inside that. Leave the center blank. God knows the target. Come back to the rings when this season has passed and fill in the target God had for you.

12

RESTING IN THE RAIN

#BlessedMode

In Mark 4, Jesus was teaching by a lake. So many people had gathered that He got in a boat and went into the water to teach from there. He taught parables and answered many questions from His disciples. As evening came that day, Jesus told the disciples to get in the boat so they could travel to the other side of the lake.

As they began sailing, a storm whipped up across the waters, and it was *furious*. The disciples began to panic. As the storm raged and tossed the boat around, waves crashed over the sides and into the boat. The disciples feared that death was on the way.

But Jesus wasn't panicking alongside them. He was sleeping on a cushion at the back of the boat. Sleeping! While the boat was filling with water! The disciples woke Him up. "How are You sleeping during this storm? Don't You care if we drown?"

Jesus got up and calmed the storm by saying, "Peace, be still!" (v. 39 NKJV). Then He turned to the disciples. "Why are you so scared? What happened to your faith?"

The disciples were shook. And now they were experiencing a different kind of fear: awe. This Man, this Teacher, could calm a storm. "Who is this? Even the wind and the waves obey him!" (v. 41).

You might be in the middle of a storm of your own right now, tossed across the waves, fearful, feeling like your boat is taking on water. But remind yourself of this story when you feel like your ship is about to sink. You've probably seen people who have a deep peace during life's difficulties. It may even seem like it's not raining on them. That kind of peace makes sense *only* because of Jesus. We can learn to rest while in the storm too, holding on to our joy and peace and not panicking—because Jesus is in control.

#LevelUpYourFaith

I look to You, Lord. I want to know what Your reaction is so that I can do exactly that in every situation. I want to be more like You, Jesus, today and every day. Help me to not lean on my own understanding. In Jesus' name I pray, amen.

#GoGetThemBlessings

God has a way of getting our attention through nature. It may be strong winds and rain, like Jesus and the disciples faced on the boat. Or a thunderstorm with lightning bolts electrifying the sky. Or it may be a sunny day with no clouds in sight. Go outside and take note of the weather. Pay attention to the breeze, the sky, the temperature, and see how God is in control of it all. Rest in that.

WARM WINDS

we do not have a high Priest who cannot sympathize with our
weaknesses, but was in all points tempted as we are, yet without
sin. Let us therefore come boldly to the throne of grace, that
we may obtain mercy and find grace to help in time of need.
HEBREWS 4:15–16 NKJV

#BlessedMode

I was getting ready to take my youngest daughter on a walk, and
the wind was really blowing outside. I figured it might be chilly,
so I grabbed her hoodie and zipped it up to the top. I put on a
hoodie too, and we headed for the door.

"Why do you have on a hoodie? It's ninety degrees outside,"
my wife said.

I looked at her like she was crazy. "No way is it that hot, not
with the way those trees are blowing."

"Well, it says it's ninety, and the forecast said wind can blow
while it's warm. But *feel* for yourself, I guess."

I trust my wife, so we took off our hoodies and headed outside. It was windy, but it was a soft, warm wind that felt amazing.
My eyes had deceived me! I saw something that looked familiar
and made an assumption. Even though I've been in Los Angeles
for many years (I grew up in Chicago), *wind* still meant cold to
me. My wife's encouragement reminded me that my eyes can't
always comprehend the whole story.

Some of us need to experience things for ourselves before we
can understand another perspective. Sometimes circumstances
aren't what they appear or our history causes us to make hasty
conclusions. And as that windy day revealed, the whole story isn't
always what we expect.

Often, we're so focused on our agenda or perspective that we miss others' feelings completely. So take the time to be present and examine where others are coming from. How can you show real love if you won't work to understand how others' feelings? Jesus was the ultimate example of empathy. He lowered Himself to experience the feelings of humankind—He felt our pain, wept with us, extended endless compassion, and ultimately died on the cross to save us all. Now *that's* empathy.

Is there a circumstance you've concluded is a certain way because previous experience? Step outside the door of your heart and feel for yourself. Be open to understanding how someone is really feeling. And feel the warm winds of true empathy and love blow over your heart and your relationships.

#LevelUpYourFaith

Lord, teach me to love others like You do, to listen with my heart so that I can respond in an empathetic, loving way, to understand others better so that my response builds people up and doesn't tear them down, and they grow closer to You. In Jesus' name I pray, amen.

#GoGetThemBlessings

God is *always* present. When we speak, He listens. How can you be present today the way God is? In a conversation, be the reason someone feels welcomed, seen, and heard. Don't think about what you'll say next. Listen with an empathetic ear and respond with love.

BACK TO THE PRESENT

#BlessedMode

When I was young, a movie came out called *Back to the Future*. I'm sure most of you have seen it. A teenager named Marty McFly (dope name, right?) is friends with a scientist named Doc. Doc is a bit eccentric and thinks he has figured out time travel. He wants to send Marty to the past to test it out.

Well, it works. Marty ends up in the past, when his parents are teenagers and before they've fallen in love. And that's when things get weird. Marty's mom thinks he's the cool new kid in town and ends up with a crush on him (yikes). Marty ends up standing up to his dad's bully, getting into some other shenanigans, and leaving quite a mark on a time in history he shouldn't even be participating in.

As events transpire, Marty realizes his actions have consequences—they're directly affecting *his own future*. If he doesn't make sure that history repeats itself, he might not even be born. In one iconic scene, Marty's body literally begins to fade as his future seems doomed.

Some people are a lot like Marty McFly: they keep going back to their past and they get stuck there. *If I had just done this or that, I'd be doing better now.* Or they feel guilty: *If only I hadn't done such-and-such, I'd be blessed now.* Some people can be so consumed by the past that they end up with intense anxiety about the future, worrying that they'll repeat the past or ruin any hopeful future. Like Marty, parts of them can begin to slowly fade—their hopes, dreams, presence with the people they love, focus on priorities. What a sad way to drift away from our beautiful lives.

Unlike Marty, we can't go back in time to fix or change the past. You may wish some things had gone differently. We all do. The key is not to dwell on them . . . and to learn. But you know what we have far beyond a time-traveling car? Peace in knowing that our future is secure and blessed because the Lord is in control. So join Him in this present moment and praise Him for the future He has planned for you.

#LevelUpYourFaith

I am blessed. My future is blessed. My children's children will be blessed. I am blessed when I come and when I go. With each passing day, I prosper because of the grace You give me, Lord! My future is secure in Your hands. In Jesus' name I pray, amen.

#GoGetThemBlessings

Write a letter to your future self—encouraging words, stories you want to remind your future self, things you hope you will have accomplished. How do you feel as you write this letter? Inspired? Hopeful? Motivated? Seal it in an envelope and date it. Two months from now, a year from now—it's up to you. I can't wait to hear how it feels when you open this letter in the future.

Jesus told him, "Stand up, roll up your sleeping mat and go on home!"
JOHN 5:8 TLB

#BlessedMode

SEEING THROUGH THE FOG

If you are willing to listen, Jesus will tell you if He is not pleased with a certain habit or way you are living. Good parents do the same for their kids, and good friends do the same for people they care about. They will give a warning or advice. Have you ever gotten into something bad that you could have prevented by listening to the people God was using to stop you from getting into a fog of lies and distractions?

Fog is hard to see through, and if it is a really thick fog, you will not be able to see what is up ahead. But thank God for fog lights! Fog lights illuminate the road beneath the fog and are used when it is difficult to see while driving.

When I was lost because of bad mistakes and choices, it felt like I was trapped in a thick fog of sin that I had entered because of my own foolish ways. Life got to be a heavy, dense fog I could not see my way out of. My vision was blurred, and everything had the potential to be harmful to me because I could not see what was coming. But oh, the joy I felt when I decided to say, "God, I want You in everything. I want You to be a part of everything. I surrender it all. Save me and show me what You have for me." I asked Him to take a hand in every area of my life.

When I focused on God, I was delighted to see Him through the fog! He changed my life. It was like seeing fog lights on a luxury sports vehicle, coming through the fog to scoop me up. And there was Jesus at the wheel, saying, "Hop in, kid. Put the seat back, and let's do this right."

God's voice is like fog lights coming to the rescue. The point is to observe and pay attention to the *voice of God*! You do not want to go through life not being able to understand why things are happening to you, searching through the fog. Get clarity spiritually. Hear the voice of God and walk toward His light.

#LevelUpYourFaith

Lord, help me see You when it is hard to see my way out. Fix my focus, fix my thoughts, and fix my ears to hear Your voice in the ones You use to give me good advice. I look to You today! Be in everything that I do. I surrender all to You. In Jesus' name I pray, amen.

#GoGetThemBlessings

Take a minute and focus on this quote: "Maybe it's not always about trying to fix something broken. Maybe it's about starting over and creating something better." What is something in your life that feels messy and hard to see a way through? How can you think of the situation with spiritual clarity and start over with God on your side?

16

ASK ANYTHING

> "If a son asks for bread from any father among you, will he give him a stone? Or if he asks for a fish, will he give him a serpent instead of a fish?"
> **LUKE 11:11 NKJV**

#BlessedMode

Can you ask God about anything and everything? Yes, and you should make a habit of it.

Think of it this way: depending on what type of parents or teachers you had growing up, you would have to ask certain things because you were a kid. "Can I stay up late?" "Can I go out with so-and-so?" "Why can't I drive to that party?" Your parents, teachers, and other adults would help you with everything you asked, wanted, or were just curious about—but you would have to ask politely, respectfully.

You asked because you were under their roof or in their care. Now, the answer to your question could be a yes or a no, but if you had a good parent, teacher, or grown-up, they gave you an answer based on wisdom and protection for your well-being. Because they cared about you, they would give you what you needed and answer in your best interest, like the father who gives bread instead of a stone, or a fish instead of a serpent. Perhaps they knew what could happen to you because of their own experience. Perhaps they responded with protection, safety, and love for you. Even if you did not like the answer, they wanted to protect you on your journey of figuring it out.

That is what God is doing for us every day! He is protecting His children; He wants to protect us from harm while we are here on earth, but we have to seek Him and ask questions before we make a move. He is our heavenly Father, and we are His children. Go to Him with every issue, and surrender all to Him. Ask Him anything and let Him save you.

Dear Lord, I do not know the consequences up ahead for the choices I make, but I know You know. And if I let You be a part of my choices— if I respond in a righteous way—I will receive a positive outcome no matter what happens. So today I decree and declare that I will ask You anything and everything that I have questions about and am curious about. In Jesus' name I pray, amen.

#GoGetThemBlessings

Remember some good advice that was given to you by a loving adult when you were a kid. Thank God for using that person to give you that advice. Now post the advice on social media to help someone else today, shout out the person who gave you the advice, and thank them for letting God use them.

17

And no wonder, since Satan himself
masquerades as an angel of light.
2 CORINTHIANS 11:14 AMP

THE BRIGHTEST LIGHT

#BlessedMode

Moths love flames, right? You've heard of the saying "like a moth to a flame"—it is a metaphor for a fatal attraction. It means, yes, something got your attention, and you're curious—but if you follow it and get too close, things could get fatal.

Like many flying insects, moths are able to find their way partly by using light as a compass. When that is the sun or the moon, it keeps them in a straight line. But when another light like a fire or candle is close by, it grabs their attention. And using instinct, the moth thinks, *Oh, follow the bright, shiny thing*, but it could be a bug zapper or a flame that could burn them up.

Imagine you are a moth, and you are focused on a light, and then someone waves another light on the right or left side of you, distracting your peripheral vision. You might look at the new light and get off course. As you focus on it, moving closer to it, you are compelled to figure out if this is friend or foe, pleasant or harmful. You don't know, and before you figure it out, *zap*! You get burned by this light.

Do not get distracted by all the lights, and I say *all* of the lights because there are many that the Enemy uses to distract us. Some will look really shiny and bright and will tempt us to follow after them. But everything that glitters isn't gold. Everything that looks precious and true might not be so. You could also say it this way: everything that glitters isn't from God. We want everything God has to give us. That is why getting wisdom and discernment is key—they keep us from following lights that could lead to harm and destruction.

There is only one light that you need to focus on, the brightest light, which is God.

Lord, when everything around me is trying to pull my focus away from Your light, help me to stay under Your spotlight. Give me the right understanding so I won't be confused by false light that does nothing for me. I want to be under Your powerful light that exposes all the darkness, and evil cannot be a part of it. Search me today, Lord. Shine Your light on me. I want to make sure everything I do and think is of You today. In Jesus' name I pray, amen.

#GoGetThemBlessings

Wait until evening. Grab a pencil, paper, Scotch tape, and a flashlight. Write on the paper this Bible verse from John 3:20: "Everyone who does evil hates the light, and will not come into the light for fear that their deeds will be exposed." Then take the paper and tape it on a wall. Turn the lights off in your room, and then turn the flashlight on, scanning the walls of the room until you reach the paper with the verse on it. Shine your light on the verse and thank God for loving you and helping you out of trouble.

18

IT'S OKAY TO SAY NO

Peace I leave with you, my peace I give to you. Not as the world gives do I give to you. Let not your hearts be troubled, neither let them be afraid."
JOHN 14:27 ESV

#BlessedMode

If you're anything like me, you have a hard time saying no. I'm naturally a people pleaser, which can be good at times—but at other times, it causes me to run dry and burn out. It's okay to say no sometimes and to not always be a people pleaser. You have a choice. If you need to work on yourself first before helping others, do that. It will help you and everyone else in the long run.

You know when you fly in a plane, and the flight attendants give the safety speech before you take off? If the plane were to depressurize and oxygen levels got too low, oxygen masks above the seat would drop down. My favorite part of the spiel is when they tell you to put on your oxygen mask before you help someone else. They advise you to take care of yourself before assisting others, because otherwise you might pass out before you can help them. You are no help if you can't breathe!

Think of that before you decide to help someone. Are you fully capable of taking on this task, and are you able to breathe comfortably while carrying it out? How is your mental state? It's not selfish to say no if you need to care of and honor yourself first. Find peace, keep it, then help others do the same.

You may be overwhelmed. Maybe that is why you have been snappy to others or angry. Maybe God is saying to you today, "Let Me help you let go of some things." Let Him take those things. He can handle your trouble, and He can handle your fears. Give them to Him and be free of them today so you can work on yourself. Add more of His peace and love to your heart, and you will discover that by finding your own peace and happiness, you won't feel overwhelmed when helping others. This will enable you to be a blessing to yourself and others.

#LevelUpYourFaith

When trouble from the world comes, I know that You protect me from it, Lord, so I will not be afraid. You give me peace, and I thank You for that! Thank You for giving me solace in times of trouble, knowing that I can rely on You and the peace that You give. Thank You, Lord. In Jesus' name I pray, amen.

#GoGetThemBlessings

Create a good vibe. Start by making a creative outlet list. If you are under stress today, express your feelings through a creative outlet—like painting, drawing, or writing—and after you are done, cross it off your list. This list will be a visual reminder that you chose to release your feelings of stress by doing something positive and productive, and you allowed God to adjust your perspective and focus.

19

We are ambassadors for Christ, as though God were pleading through us: we implore you on Christ's behalf, be reconciled to God.
2 CORINTHIANS 5:20 NKJV

CAMPAIGNING FOR JESUS

Have you seen an anti-smoking commercial recently? These were really popular in the nineties, when a lot of people still smoked. The commercials act as warnings to smokers, a reminder of the harm they are doing to their bodies. A recent commercial I saw had a scientist blowing air into two different lungs on display outside of the body to show smokers the harm they are doing to the inside of their bodies. The lung of the smoker was shriveled up and didn't expand to its full potential when air was put in it. The lung of the nonsmoker looked healthy and expanded fully. The producers behind this commercial are hoping that the smokers watching it will be affected by this serious message, will let go of their tobacco habit, and will make better choices for their health.

Similarly, believers are like a commercial for God's love, an anti-evil ad campaign. As believers, we want our anti-evil campaign to affect people living in sin and influence them to choose to follow Christ. We are a constant commercial for them, showing that Jesus saves those who follow Him. We don't want anyone to perish! We want everyone to have life and have it abundantly, to be reconciled to God.

Because we are Christ's ambassadors, we must stay encouraged as we share our faith, no matter the dirty looks or the hate we receive. Because we love Jesus, we must continue to pray for others, that they will give up the sin that is bringing them down. Just like those anti-smoking campaigns, we have a message that will bring others health, life, and a better future.

Lord, I will let everyone know what You have done in my life so they can know that the same can happen for them. The name of Jesus is advertised when people see me. I pray that they see Your glory working in me! In Jesus' name I pray, amen.

#GoGetThemBlessings

Let's make a commercial, a campaign for God's love: "Hi. I'm_____. First, I'd like to give honor and praise to our Lord Jesus Christ, who is the head of my life. God is awesome! He is always here to help me and to guide me. He shows me love, and I trust in Him. I trust His Word, and I will let people know about His grace and love. I am an ambassador for Christ, and I approve this message." What would your commercial sound like?

20

You keep him in perfect peace whose mind is
stayed on you, because he trusts in you.
ISAIAH 26:3 ESV

#BlessedMode

Be mindful of your mind. When our minds are at peace, we can hear from God, enjoy His presence, and rest in His promises. When our minds are filled with doubt, depression, or negativity, it's harder to feel and know the peace God wants to give us. How is your mind today? Where are you at right now?

Mental health awareness is so important and allows us to open up about our emotions, anxiety, and problems—and how we deal with them. Do you suppress your problems, process them, or leave them in the past? You do not want to lose your mind because of past choices, past abuse, or past mistakes.

And these are not things you can easily sweep under a rug. Have you ever seen something obviously hidden under a rug? It becomes a distracting lump. The rug is not level, and you can tell something is there.

It's the same as when we try to hide the hurt or the emotions that are overwhelming us. The things that plague our minds become more obvious. Stress shows on our faces. Negative emotions drain our energy. Doubt and depression can lead to broken relationships, harm to ourselves, suicidal thoughts, and a host of terrible things. We do not want that. To be able to do what God put us here to do, we need to take our mental health seriously and deal with it in healthy, positive ways.

Instead of hiding your issues, work on resolving them. Talk to a friend or your pastor. Get the proper help you need so your mind and heart are not packed with heaviness or things that keep you from joy. God loves you, and He wants to keep you in His perfect peace.

God, You are awesome. You know the things from my past that I need to let go of. You know the thoughts I have that need to be untangled so I can put my thoughts on You. Thank You for Your grace. In Jesus' name I pray, amen.

#GoGetThemBlessings

Everything you need has been given to you by God. Keep moving and let your faith work! Say, "I am fully capable to make it happen, with God's help." And know that it will happen! Add today's scripture to your prayer time. Pray it specifically over your circumstances and make it personal: "You keep **me** in perfect peace. **My** mind is stayed on You, because I trust in You, Lord, with _____." Let that sink into your spirit for a few moments, and then say it again.

21

[Wisdom's] ways are ways of pleasantness, and all her paths are peace.

PROVERBS 3:17 ESV

MASTER PEACE

#BlessedMode

I love the saying, "I'm a masterpiece trying to master peace." The first time I heard this, it nearly brought me to tears because it is so true: we are each a walking, beautiful work of art made by God, trying to find some type of peace on our journey.

With all that is going on in the world, anxiety is at an all-time high. Maybe you've tried to forget the turmoil of 2020—a global pandemic, political animosity, civil unrest, unemployment levels off the charts. What a crazy year, full of stress! Most of us are still dealing with the chaos. Restlessness and uncertainty are running rampant in the streets.

I have learned that when I react to stress with negative emotions instead of peace, things only become more stressful. I need a peaceful mindset to give me strength and comfort each day. So I search for peace—not just to find it but to master it. And it's not just me. I see others who need relief from pain, who need peace, and I want to help them as well. We all want and need peace—tranquility, freedom from chaos, quietness, security, and calmness.

So how do we find peace in the chaos? The Bible verse for today says that wisdom will lead you to peace. When there is trouble on every side, seek wisdom. When you detect a disturbance of peace going on in your life, focus on God's wise words. It will take work, but you can master peace. To become a master at something, you must first become a student, studying to get the proper knowledge and understanding. So we should study peace and ways to defeat the chaos of the mind. And then we put what we've learned into practice. We stop trying to control chaotic situations in life—they are out of our control anyway!—and we learn how to control our thoughts and behaviors. This will bring peace.

#LevelUpYourFaith

Dear Lord, teach me how to study! Teach me how to pay attention to techniques and plans that help me keep my peace today and every day. You are Master over everything I do. I am Your humble student, heavenly Father. Teach me more of Your ways, and I will keep them. In Jesus' name I pray, amen.

#GoGetThemBlessings

Make a peace plan. Maybe it involves breathing exercises or a specific prayer or a worship song. Control your response to stressful circumstances by planning ahead. When you choose a peaceful way of thinking, that is exactly what you will get. Plan for peace, and honor God and yourself by protecting your peace. What are some ways you can bring more peace to difficult situations?

22

TAKE IT BACK

God, your God, will restore everything you lost; he'll have compassion on you; he'll come back and pick up the pieces from all the places where you were scattered.
DEUTERONOMY 30:3 MSG

#BlessedMode

Have you ever had a smartphone that needed to be repaired or restored because you cracked the screen? It sucks!

One time during a workout, I wanted to get these new calisthenics moves on video so I could post to my social media. I balanced my phone on the pull-up bar. As soon as I pressed record and started the exercise, the phone fell to the ground hard, crashing with an alarming sound. My heart dropped. Broken pieces were scattered all over. I had made a dumb choice. I knew the phone wasn't secure, but I did it anyway.

When I took it to be repaired, they said they'd have my phone for a few hours, but it would be like new after. I started having withdrawal symptoms. No joke! I'd reach into my pocket . . . but no phone. When I finally picked it up, the phone was indeed like new, and all my contacts, messages, notes, and photos were there. Everything was given back to me. Yeah, I had made a mistake, but the repair shop returned it to me better than before, and with new protection (a screen protector) if it ever fell again.

Now, I've made mistakes *way* worse than breaking a phone, things that changed the course of my life in the wrong direction. But afterward, I prayed, *Lord, help me fix this*, and He did! He restored my life and made me new, better, prepared for future challenges.

When you trust in God, He won't let the Enemy take your

peace, your joy, or your faith. Everything the devil has stolen will be given back, with the Lord's help. If you have lost your way somehow, turn back to the One who created you and saved you. He will restore you to better than before! You will be made new. Nothing is impossible for God!

#LevelUpYourFaith

Thank You, Lord, for giving everything back! Today, I stomp on the devil's head! I am better each day because I trust in You, Lord. I have my faith, I have my joy, and I have my happiness because of You! In Jesus' name I pray, amen.

#GoGetThemBlessings

There is a song by the great gospel singer Dorinda Clark-Cole called "Take It Back" that I recommend. Maybe you've had a hard season and it feels like the devil has stolen your joy. But guess what? He can't keep it! God is still king. He is on the throne, and the devil is defeated! Trust that God will make things new. Thank Him for the change that is coming!

23

GOD'S MASTERPIECE

#BlessedMode

I want you to be aware of the bigger plan, the bigger picture for your life. Remember that you are a masterpiece, beautifully and wonderfully made by God (Psalm 139:14). What God put in you is what makes you beautiful—what is inside, what is beneath the skin, what is in your heart. We are spirits underneath it all. Let your joy and peace in believing be on display in your life as if you were transparent, so people can see God in you and be affected by it so much that they find hope in Him as well.

When an artist creates a painting, people gravitate toward what is inside the frame, not the frame itself. Before the artwork is ever put in a frame or hung on a wall, the artist has a vision or message they want to share, which they then paint on the canvas.

The same goes for you and me. God created us with a purpose and a message to share with others. It's a message of love and hope, joy and peace. Let your inner peace and joy from God shine like fresh paint on a canvas. The frame is just what's on the outside. You are special to God—a unique work of art.

#LevelUpYourFaith

I belong to You, Lord! I am reminded today that You created me for a purpose, and as I grow closer to You, I pray that You reveal to me the details of that purpose and put me on the right path to manifest it. In Jesus' name I pray, amen.

#GoGetThemBlessings

Visit an art museum. You can go to one in person or visit one virtually. Or take a look at the art on the walls of your house. Whichever option you pick, as you look at the artwork, pay attention to the message the artist is giving in the painting and the name of the painting. Then, remember that you are a walking work of art with a name and a message. Think of all the people God has created, each with a different message of joy and peace—all masterpieces.

24

PERSIST

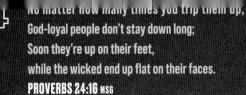

No matter how many times you trip them up,
God-loyal people don't stay down long;
Soon they're up on their feet,
while the wicked end up flat on their faces.
PROVERBS 24:16 MSG

#BlessedMode

As you work toward your goals, know that you cannot please everybody. Some people are so self-absorbed that they only think about themselves and really do not care about your opinion or your feelings in the matter. These people offer no advice, just mean opinions. Do not let their negative comments derail your dreams. Do not stop to please them. Your dream and your goal are just that: *your* dream and *your* goal. Pursue them for you, to better yourself.

Depending on the goal you are trying to reach, it could feel like an uphill battle. But you are keeping your joy through the blood, sweat, and tears because, bit by bit, you are seeing results. Don't allow negative words from other people stifle your growth. Maybe you start a new workout routine and feel good about it, but one of your hateful family members or friends says something like, "You've been working out, but you look the same to me. I don't think it is showing." Don't let their words keep you from the progress you're making to feel better and be healthier. Or, they might hate on you going to church, saying things like, "You still go to that church every Sunday and to that Bible study after work? It's not going to change you for the better." But you know that building spiritual habits and fellowship is important to spiritual growth. Having faith while goal-seeking is important if you're going to get to the blessing.

You can stay persistent! You can lay a foundation and finish the work. You can prove it to yourself and meet the goal, confirming the Word of God, which proclaimed that you could do it. Now you're a testimony and motivation for others. The haters will just move on to the next person, trying to stop them from achieving their goals because they see that their hate had no effect on your progress. Your reward is on the way, but you have to stay in it. Keep up the great work. God's got you!

#LevelUpYourFaith

Dear Lord, I put my faith in You as I pursue my dreams and goals. You are with me every step of the way. I know You will not leave me, and You will provide me all the strength I need, ministering to me along the way. All my dreams will come true when they are from You. They are an example of how beautifully You work in my life! Thank You, Lord. In Jesus' name I pray, amen.

#GoGetThemBlessings

What are some of your goals? When do you want to achieve them? Create a schedule working back from this date, and break up your plan into small sections, each with its own reward and goal. Celebrate the small wins and little victories.

25

TOTALLY CROSSED OUT

> Then Jesus told his disciples, "If anyone would come after me, let him deny himself and take up his cross and follow me."
> **MATTHEW 16:24** ESV

The other day I was listening to a nineties album from the hip-hop duo Kris Kross. Their debut multiplatinum album was called *Totally Krossed Out*. They posed on the front of the album with their baggy jeans and baseball jerseys on backward. I was a fan of this album, so playing it brought back good memories; but as I listened to them say "totally krossed out," I thought, *That is a word*. Funny how replacing a C with a K can change the meaning entirely. Instead of hearing the line as an amusing play on words, I heard the expression as it relates to faith.

As Christians, once we give our life to Christ, and we become His disciples, we must be "totally crossed out" to follow Him. We have to deny ourselves and pick up our cross, as He said in Matthew 16:24. To be crossed out for Christ means we must endure whatever may come. We must also be willing to make sacrifices in our lives, which will involve not doing all the crazy things we used to do. You may have to cross out some old habits in your life to live a new life in Christ. And when people see you, they'll see Christ, so you'll have to play the background instead of the foreground.

When you walk with Christ, you have to *carry the cross totally crossed out*. It's like you have to sit down with Jesus, holding a big, red, permanent spiritual Sharpie in your hand, and let Him evaluate the things you are doing in your life that need to be crossed out. Mistakes you need to cross out of your memory bank and stop dwelling on. Habits, generational curses—they all need to be *totally crossed out*. And that's not easy. God might want you to cross out something that, being human, you do not want to give up. But spiritually it's good for you. And notice how I said *you* hold the Sharpie because *you* have to do it. You have to cross it out. Take action and cross out the things in your life that keep you from God.

#LevelUpYourFaith

Lord, I want people to see You when they see me. I choose to follow You. I will let go of and cross out the things that You disapprove of. Help me recognize these things so I can totally cross them out from my life. In Jesus' name I pray, amen.

#GoGetThemBlessings

Download the song "Jump," by Kris Kross or play it on YouTube. No, this is not a worship song, but it will get you jumping—and as you jump, think of everything we said about God today in this passage. Have fun! You're in Blessed Mode!

26

REAL FRIENDS

One who has unreliable friends soon comes to ruin, but
there is a friend who sticks closer than a brother.
PROVERBS 18:24

#BlessedMode

"Fake friends are no different than shadows; they stick around during your brightest moments but disappear during your darkest moments." This quote is so true! You can always see a shadow when the light is bright. You can wave at it and talk to it if you want. People might think you're crazy, but you can have some great times with your shadow. *This shadow is going everywhere with me. It's like my best friend or something.* But then a storm hits and clouds cover the sun. Where is your shadow now? When trouble comes into your life, where are the friends or the family members who were by your side in the good times?

Now, some friends *will* remain with you in the storm and *will* be there to encourage you. These are real friends. But I'm talking about the fake ones, the ones who suddenly disappear when circumstances are different and life gets hard. Maybe a friend who used to stick around in the storm has deceived you somehow. They used to be there for you, but now it isn't playing out the same way. You feel abandoned and hurt, alone in the storm. *Now what should I do? I'm all alone in this!*

That is the time when you call out to Jesus, friend. Because He is there in the sunshine and in the storm. Jesus is there no matter what is happening. He will never leave you. He is a friend who sticks closer than a brother.

When Jesus speaks to you, let it edify your spirit. Work on your perspective by choosing God's perspective. In these moments,

His perspective can pull you out of your disappointment and fear and help you find the light in the storm. His presence is like a rainbow in the sky, a bright moon on a dark night, a promise to always be by your side there and that you will live through this.

God loves you, so take hold of His hand and push through it. Oh, what a friend we have in Jesus!

#LevelUpYourFaith

Lord, I am so happy I can call You my friend! Help me to love more, to be more understanding, to forgive others, and to trust You more each day. I thank You for the real friends You've brought along on this journey, and for future friends You will reveal to me. In Jesus' name I pray, amen.

#GoGetThemBlessings

Go for a walk. Let the rhythm of your steps calm you. Enjoy the solitude with just you and your thoughts. Take time to breathe and think. Let God minister to you as you are free from all distraction. Enjoy the walk with just you and God under the sun.

27

A LIFE OF GIFTS

Every good and perfect gift is from above, coming down from the Father of the heavenly lights, who does not change like shifting shadows.
JAMES 1:17

#BlessedMode

Life is a gift from God, and love is a gift from God. Every day you wake up should feel like your birthday, Christmas, Thanksgiving, and New Year's Day all rolled into one with God by your side, bringing you life, relationships, people to love, and daily blessings. And every time you take a breath, you should be reminded of these gifts and celebrate.

There is a delightful video of Stevie Wonder talking about the gifts of life and love at a wedding. He sits down at the piano with a newlywed couple, both of them smiling ear to ear at him, overjoyed that Stevie is about to sing at their reception. Before he begins to sing, he shares a loving message with the couple and the crowd: "The greatest thing in life is love, and the greatest thing in love is life. They were both created by the greatest thing I know, which is God! It is always a wonderful thing to celebrate God's blessings of life and love." Then he starts to sing his legendary classic "Ribbon in the Sky," which has a beautiful lyric about God. There are such awesome words and messages in that song. Go listen to it. I think you'll be encouraged.

When things get rough, look up and imagine a ribbon in the sky like a beautiful bow! As you look up, be reminded that love and life are perfect gifts from our heavenly Father above and that He loves you endlessly.

Hallelujah!

#LevelUpYourFaith

Thank You, Lord, for the gift of life. I'm so grateful for each day You give me. Thank You, Lord, for the gift of love and how You remind me of Your love. I know that every good and perfect gift comes from You. All the things that I am thankful for and that are dear to my heart are gifts from You, and again I thank You. In Jesus' name I pray, amen.

#GoGetThemBlessings

Sit down with a pen and a paper, and write down five things you are grateful for. Think about these five things, and when you get that good feeling of gratitude in your body, sit with it for a few minutes more, enjoying the blessing.

28

KEEP TRAINING

You need to persevere so that when you have done the will of God, you will receive what he has promised.
HEBREWS 10:36

#BlessedMode

We must train our faith to strengthen our spiritual muscles, and it's not much different from the way we might train our physical muscles to prepare for a race or as part of a regular fitness and health routine. When we want to strengthen our physical muscles, we put the work in. We might go to a gym and talk to a trainer who can help us train properly. The trainer might say something like, "Today we're going to strengthen your upper body by doing compound lifts so your body can endure heavy lifting." Compound lifts are exercises that use several muscle groups at the same time, and they'll help you with balance and coordination while you build strength. And they work!

We need the same kind of training for our spiritual muscles—exercises that work multiple spiritual muscle groups. Our goal in our faith is to be stronger so we're able to handle the heavy weights that might come our way in life and still be in proper balance with God. More than just being spiritually strong, we want to be able to persevere, to endure!

You may have gone through some tough times. I sure have. In those moments, sometimes our first response is to scream out, "Lord, how do I endure this?" The good news is that strength builds upon strength, so you have hope and a plan.

So how do we train our faith? How do we grow in strength and endurance? Faith comes by hearing the Word of God (Romans 10:17). When you're in church, you hear God's Word, but what about the other days? How do you train Monday through Saturday? We need to edify and strengthen our spirits by reading the Word of God every day, alone or in connection with other believers through small groups, Bible studies, and more. As we develop a consistent routine of hearing and applying the Word of God, those spiritual muscles are strengthened—with faith built upon faith.

A big part of this is also talking to yourself the right way. What are you saying to yourself consistently? Are you speaking words of life to your own heart, proclaiming God's hand in your life, shouting out the things He has done in your life? Are you consistently in study, prayer and speech strengthening your spiritual muscles to be able to persevere? God gave you ultimate victory on the cross, so keep training! When the time comes, you'll be ready to go the distance.

#LevelUpYourFaith

Lord, give me words that will motivate me to train my faith, and help me say words that will give me the power to endure. Your words bring life—the best life, a blessed life. Thank You for showing me how to tap in to my spiritual strength today. In Jesus' name I pray, amen.

#GoGetThemBlessings

Meditate on scripture that talks about endurance, such as: "We also glory in our sufferings, because we know that suffering produces perseverance" (Roman 5:3) and "Be joyful in hope, patient in affliction, faithful in prayer" (Romans 12:12). Make note of these and put them on your wall where you will see them as a daily reminder to persevere!

29

Cause me to hear Your lovingkindness in the
morning, for in You do I trust.
PSALM 143:8 NKJV

CAN YOU HEAR ME NOW?

Back in 2002, Verizon Wireless launched a commercial campaign
called "Can You Hear Me Now?" A Verizon employee, the Test
Man, would go to great lengths to make sure his customers could
hear him clearly on their wireless devices.

The first commercial kicked off with him on his cell in China,
asking, "Can you hear me now?"

He'd wait for the answer, then reply, "Good."

Then this Verizon dude started popping up all over the world
asking the same question—at the top of a mountain, walking
through a corn field, in a busy office, wandering in a rainforest
or desert.

"Can you hear me now?"

"Good."

The voiceover would say, "No matter where you go, your call
goes through. Verizon Wireless. We never stop working for you."

I have some pretty amazing news, guys. Our connection to
God is better, clearer, and closer than *any* wireless connection—
even if we're on the top of Mount Everest. God wants us to stay
connected to Him so He can speak to us and speak into the purpose He has for us. You were born for a purpose beyond what you
can imagine, with the "connection" of the Holy Spirit revealing
His will and power in miracles and blessings all around you.

God wants us to be sure that our connection is clear, that we
can hear Him and His lovingkindess. How do we do that? We

read our Bibles. We pray. We praise Him. And when God says, "Can you hear Me now?" our response is, "Yes, Lord! Good!"

No matter where you go in life, your call will always go through. God is listening for you, ready to take your call.

30

THE ULTIMATE GPS

When I got my driver's license, my dad and I made an agreement: I could drive his car to school as long as I got up early enough to drop him off at the train station and picked him up on time after work. This was awesome for sixteen-year-old Kel. I had some *wheels*. And all I had to do was keep our agreement.

One day, a friend asked for a ride to his girlfriend's house. I figured it was close, so I told him to hop in. Everything changed when he told me to turn onto the highway. I had just gotten my license and wasn't comfortable with the highway.

"Let me drive," he said. "I'll get us there quicker."

We were already far from my neighborhood, and I needed to pick up my dad, so I agreed. We passed *finally* got off the highway, making right turns, left turns, even some U-turns.

I had no idea how to get back. I looked at the time and panicked. I had no cell phone, and there wasn't any GPS in those days, so I had to look for a familiar street. I finally spotted something familiar: a cemetery I knew was in my grandmother's neighborhood, close to home. But I must have stared at it a bit too long. *BANG!* I hit the back of the car in front of me.

A gangster-looking dude jumped out the car. "Aye, little homie, you just hit my car!" he yelled. He banged on the window, and I climbed out cautiously. He could have a gun.

I looked at our cars. I didn't see any damage. Neither did he. "Both cars look cool though. I think you good."

He hopped in his car and sped off. My heart was beating through my chest. I got back in my dad's car and started racing through the streets again, trying to make up for lost time. But I was still lost. I might as well have been driving with a blindfold on. By the grace of God, I made it in enough time to see my dad walking out of the L station. Have you ever felt lost in life? Like you don't know where to turn next? With every turn, you get into more trouble. If I had stopped panicking and stopped to ask for directions, I would've been okay. But I allowed fear to take over and made the wrong decisions.

Think about your life like a car. You've been given the key to your life from your heavenly Father. And He has laid out a plan. You just have to follow it. When you make decisions outside of God's purpose, you'll hit roadblocks. Slow down right now. Ask God, *What is Your plan for me, Lord? Which way should I turn? Lord, light my pathway!* God is the ultimate GPS. He will direct your paths.

#LevelUpYourFaith

I am in agreement with You, Lord. This means I will go wherever You want me to go! I won't be distracted or turn away from Your guidance. In Jesus' name I pray, amen.

#GoGetThemBlessings

Make a playlist of your favorite inspirational music. Then take a drive and turn on your new playlist. As you listen, imagine that the Holy Spirit is your passenger, guiding each turn.

31

THE CROSS IN THE CROSSWIND

When the day of Pentecost had come, they were all together in one place, and suddenly a sound came from heaven like a rushing violent wind, and it filled the whole house where they were sitting. There appeared to them tongues resembling fire, which were being distributed [among them], and they rested on each one of them [as each person received the Holy Spirit]. And they were all filled [that is, diffused throughout their being] with the Holy Spirit and began to speak in other tongues (different languages), as the Spirit was giving them the ability to speak out [clearly and appropriately].
ACTS 2:1-4 AMP

#BlessedMode

There are all kinds of winds. A light breeze off the ocean. Santa Ana winds. Crosswinds, which will knock you right off your feet. Crosswinds can cause turbulence for planes. They can even turn whole vehicles sideways! Troublesome or shocking situations in our lives can feel a lot like a violent crosswind knocking us over. You lose your job suddenly. Or a loved one passes away. Or something happens that sends you into a season of hardship. Those life winds can slam you sideways.

But sometimes those winds of life are also accompanied with a lesson, an opportunity for growth, an experience of grace and provision. That's why it's so important to stay calm, to focus on God at all times (even the turbulent times) and to *find the cross in the crosswind*—because it is always a blessing in the storm.

In today's verse, something amazing happened—and it happened via the wind. The Holy Spirit came down on the disciples like a violent, rushing wind and allowed them to speak in tongues, to speak in a special language from God. Can you even imagine that? (I really wonder if their screen door was latched.)

In that instance, what might have been a terrifying wind brought with it a miracle. Pay attention to the winds in your life, whether calm or powerful. God is in those winds! Worship and give Him praise as the winds of life blow.

#LevelUpYourFaith

Lord, You are our shelter from harm. Our comfort. A calming wind that breathes life into us. I will not break away from Your love and kindness. In Jesus' name I pray, amen.

#GoGetThemBlessings

Go to YouTube or your favorite streaming service, and search for relaxing wind noises. Close your eyes as you listen to how sweet the sound of wind can be, even when it's strong. Let this be a reminder to you to seek peace and shelter in God during rough winds.

32

YOUR TEMPLE

Do you not know that your bodies are temples of the Holy Spirit, who is in you, whom you have received from God? You are not your own.
1 CORINTHIANS 6:19

#BlessedMode

I stopped drinking a long time ago. I didn't want to harm my body and also wanted to be alert and focused at all times. Drinking did the opposite. Prior to stopping, I sometimes had a drink at celebrations, but I noted that if I was sad, emotional, or hurt, alcohol was an especially bad addition. It didn't give me what I was seeking—comfort from the stress of the world. And the relief was brief.

Once I stopped drinking, I discovered that I was also an emotional eater. If I had stressful day, I could drown in a bag of chips or cookies. I realized that I wanted no part of emotional consumption. These things didn't help me meet my goals, and I had seen too many family members, peers, and acquaintances pass away because of health issues related to lifestyle.

I want to be healthy and clear-headed and to live a long life with the people I love. That means taking care of my temple. And I also want inspire others to be conscious about what they put in their bodies so they can meet their goals and love their people for a long time. So I'm serious about caring for my temple and taking the right kind of control over my physical *and* spiritual self.

Today's Bible verse reminds us that we are temples of the Holy Spirit, a place for God to dwell. Our bodies are not our own. We must care for our temples—mentally, physically, and spiritually. It's interesting to me that in front of our ears is an area called the temple and that those muscles help open and close the jaw. The temple muscles act as a gateway to the temple of our bodies, letting in what we consume and letting out what we think and say. We must make sure that what we let in is edifying.

Ask yourself, *Is what I consume feeding my spirit? Is what I'm thinking righteous? When I speak, am I causing blessing and not destruction? How am I keeping my body clean for the Holy Spirit?* Now take care of that temple.

#LevelUpYourFaith

As for me and my house, we will serve the Lord. You take care of my house and my family, Lord. I will keep my house, my mind, and my spirit clean. In Jesus' name I pray, amen.

#GoGetThemBlessings

Watch what you say today. Think before you speak. Take a few seconds before you respond to make sure that your words are said with love because, as Proverbs says, "Words satisfy the mind as much as fruit does the stomach; good talk is as gratifying as a good harvest" (18:20 MSG).

33

A BEACON IN THE NIGHT

You are the light of [Christ to] the world. A city set on a hill cannot be hidden; nor does anyone light a lamp and put it under a basket, but on a lampstand, and it gives light to all who are in the house. Let your light shine before men in such a way that they may see your good deeds *and* moral excellence, and [recognize and honor and] glorify your Father who is in heaven."

MATTHEW 5:14–16 AMP

#BlessedMode

You've probably been on this kind of road trip. The hours are dragging on. It's getting late. Everyone is hungry and tired. Someone (definitely not me LOL) might be getting a little cranky as the minutes and hours pass. It feels like this trip will never end. But for miles, all you can see is darkness, not a light or even the Golden Arches in sight. You're hoping and praying that around the next bend, you'll see an exit, a light shining from the top of a fast-food restaurant or diner that signals help is near. When you finally see those familiar lights ahead, it almost feels like you're driving home. Extra fries, please!

Restaurants, especially on freeways, often have brightly lit signs, some of them a familiar logo, others just large and clear and bold so they're easy to identify. Those bright signs convey a message—what need this establishment can meet. If you're hungry, they have the solution for your hunger. But what if the lit sign is out or is broken? You'd probably miss it in the dead of night and drive right on by.

As believers, our faith should look like that brightly lit sign in the middle of a dark freeway. Those around us may be tired, hungry for hope, searching for something to fill a need. Shine your light! Make sure people know you're there and you're open to the public, ready to share the hope you have and the sustenance in Christ that truly satisfies hunger.

Be open about your love for Christ and about what He has done for you and can do for others. Many people have been on a long road of hurt, darkness, and pain. They are looking for a blessed exit to help lead them away from sin. Your shining light might be just the sign they need to signal it's time to get off the freeway. "O taste and see that the LORD is good; blessed is the man that trusteth in Him!" (Psalm 34:8 KJV).

Just imagine that weary traveler. Their blessed exit is here! With tears in their eyes and a smile on their face, they slow down. It's time to stop and let the light of God's grace fill their souls.

#LevelUpYourFaith

Lord, I will continue to be bold about my faith, showing Your love to others through my actions and the way I speak. I will continue to shine Your light, Lord, and let others know about the grace and peace You give to all who seek You. In Jesus' name I pray, amen.

#GoGetThemBlessings

Let someone know about your love for Christ today! Share your testimony, a blessing, or one of your favorite Bible verses.

34

Commit your work to the LORD, and your plans will be established.
PROVERBS 16:3 ESV

SHARED COMMITMENT

#BlessedMode

When I first started as youth pastor at my church, I had to fly out of town for a quick business trip to promote a television project I was working on. My week had already been busy, and now the weekend was going to be busy too, and I hadn't finished my sermon for Sunday morning yet. Every time I attempted to work on it before or after work, a distraction would pop up. I decided I'd work on it on the plane ride home. The four-hour flight was more than enough time to finish the sermon. But once I got on the plane, a new problem arose: I was so physically and mentally tired after working that I could barely keep my eyes open.

The captain announced that we'd land at 12 A.M. Sunday morning. If I wanted to get some sleep before church, I needed to finish my sermon in a timely fashion. I got some coffee from the flight attendant before I dove in, but that coffee did not work! I sat at my laptop with one eye open and slowly pecked away at the keys. "It's late," the flight attendant said. "Why don't you watch a movie and relax like the rest of the passengers?"

Was I tired from the work event? Absolutely. Yes. I wanted to relax! But I knew I couldn't. I had made a commitment to God and to my church. This wasn't the first time I'd had to write a sermon through the night, but I was overwhelmed. I'm sure you've been in a similar situation in your own life. So I stopped and offered up a simple prayer: *God, help me.*

I continued to study and read Bible verses, and as the minutes passed, God did just what I had prayed for: He gave me spiritual energy that helped my physical self wake up so I could prepare my sermon. God's love for me, for my church, and for the teens He teaches through me fueled my soul. I preached the next morning and thanked God for His grace in preparing me. And afterward, He spoke to me about my schedule—that I needed to commit more time to prayer and study and to release the distractions holding me back.

In those moments of exhaustion, God reminded me that *we do nothing alone.* Every talent, task, goal, and job is done by *His power* working in us. Is there an area in your life where you can see that God is asking for you to commit to a closer relationship as He comes alongside you? Praise Him for His unwavering commitment in your life.

#LevelUpYourFaith

My faith is in You, Lord. I seek Your approval above all else. I will stay committed to Your Word as I work heartily for You, not for humankind. You give me strength, so I seek Your guidance daily. In Jesus' name I pray, amen.

#GoGetThemBlessings

Before you make a decision today, search your heart. Is the choice before you filled with God's love? Do you feel His will? Ask God before moving forward with anything because you'll need Him wherever you're going next.

Trust in the LORD with all your heart and lean
not on your own understanding.
PROVERBS 3:5

35

THE REPAIR MAN

I was thinking the other day about my sketch character "the repair man," who I played on *All That.* The joke was that he would try to fix things on his own but would always mess them up worse than before he started. That is what we do sometimes. God has given us a vision and instructions on how to pursue something, but then we get impatient and try to fix or do things on our own—and we end up messing it all up!

One time I tried fixing something on my own and it didn't end well—at least not the way I was hoping. For example, something solid hits a fish tank and slowly you see a small crack or fracture. It starts forming this web of lines, radial cracks, from the point of impact. The stress lines form conchoidal fractures that are shaped like arches on the left and right sides of the point of impact, slowly breaking the glass.

It's impossible to fix. So you try to pick up this fish tank, which is going to put more stress on the glass. You try to touch it softly, but the cracks keep spreading, and the broken glass eventually shatters, water and fish spilling out at this point. It was not your intention, but by trying to fix it, you made it worse.

Now, look, you can probably clean up this mess without too much trouble. You can get another fish tank and maybe a bucket to save the fish. You can mop up the water and pick up the glass. But when something in your life is broken and you are trying to fix, it might not be easy to fix. It might stay broken.

How do you fix a broken situation? You trust in the Lord with all your heart, and you don't rely on your own abilities. You believe and trust that God will help you fix and repair the mess. Remember to trust in the Lord at all times (Psalm 62:8). God is the author and the finisher of your life (Hebrews 12:2). He knows what you need and how to fix it. God is the ultimate Repair Man!

#LevelUpYourFaith

You repair the brokenhearted, Lord. You bind up all wounds. You can change a negative situation into a positive situation—and a broken situation into a fixed one! You are the ultimate divine Repair Man, and I trust that You will work all things out for my good. In Jesus' name I pray, amen.

#GoGetThemBlessings

Grab some paper and tape. Draw a big heart on the paper, and then tear the paper right down the middle. Wait, that will ruin your great artwork! It's okay; you've done it for a reason. Grab your tape and connect the two pieces of paper, putting the heart back together. Once it's repaired, then write inside the heart, "He heals the brokenhearted." Post your art on social media and share how He has healed your heart.

Trust in the Lᴏʀᴅ with all your heart and lean
not on your own understanding.
PROVERBS 3:5

#BlessedMode

Ducks look like they're having the time of their lives floating on a lake, don't they? From above the water, all you see are beautiful feathers and bushy tails as they effortlessly float and quack along their merry way. My youngest daughter likes to call them *quack-quacks*. They look so cute, smiling and gliding along the surface of the water. But beneath the water is a different story. These little quack-quacks are paddling away with their feet and legs, often at an intensity that doesn't match the comfy and chill vibe we see from the surface. Ducks' feet have only three webbed toes, but this shape helps them slice through water and propel themselves forward.

Depending on the weather, ducks could be paddling along in comfy bathtub-warm water or at temps that are very cold or even icy. Which leads me to something very cool I found out about ducks: the blood vessels in their feet work together in a special way to protect them from heat loss. That's why they can swim in extremely cold water. Isn't that amazing? God made their bodies to be able to handle this. They're still working hard obviously, moving those legs and feet through the water, but the temperature of the water isn't harming them or slowing them down.

God created everything on the earth—you, me, birds, trees, animals, *everything*. And He knew the types of conditions, situations, or troubles that could be challenging or harmful to each and every creature, even quack-quacks. So He prepared ducks by creating them in such a way that they can be safe even harsh conditions.

God did the same thing when He created you too. He knew what conditions you might face, what challenges might come your way, and He created you to handle all of it—with Him by your side. I believe God is saying something important to you today: "I've got you. Don't worry. I'm right here by your side. You were *made* for this moment."

Is it a dream you're chasing? Is it a problem you need His help to solve? Don't be fearful. He created you for just this moment. Dive in and be submerged in His grace.

#LevelUpYourFaith

Sometimes life can feel like I'm dipping my toes in cold water, but I know, Lord, that no matter how cold this world gets, You warm my heart with your love, kindness, and grace. I will relax today knowing that You have me covered. I find refuge under Your wings of protection. Thank You, Lord. In Jesus' name I pray, amen.

#GoGetThemBlessings

Run a bath and just soak in it. Play some worship music. Relax and enjoy being still. Then invite the Holy Spirit to soak you in His presence. Focus on the Lord's presence within you. (If you don't have a bathtub, turn on the shower and let the steam from the hot water fill the room, and do the same as above.) Enjoy.

BOX UP HAPPINESS

May the God of hope fill you with all joy and peace in believing, so that by the power of the Holy Spirit you may abound in hope.
ROMANS 15:13 ESV

#BlessedMode

My youngest daughter's school asked my wife and me to make a happiness box for her—to be used if she feels upset, sad, or angry in class. Every kid in the class has one. When they need it, the teacher can bring out the happiness box with the kid's name on it, and inside are things that make the child feel happy. So what did they ask us to put in the happiness box? Pictures of family and friends smiling and having fun. Drawings that we created with our daughter, toys, musical instruments, bubbles, and other fun things we know she likes.

My wife and I enjoyed putting it together. It actually made us happy thinking of how happy it will make our daughter when she sees what is inside. We even took it up a notch. We wanted the box to also look happy on the outside, so we used a pink treasure chest for her box and put stickers of her favorite cartoon characters all over it. When we were done, we stepped back and looked at it with joy.

No parent wants their little one to be unhappy, especially if they aren't around to cheer them up in that moment. That's why the happiness box is such a good idea. God wants us to be happy too, but He knows this world can get very dark and sinful, which can distract us and hurt us at times. So He gives us instructions in the Bible, which I like to think of as His "happiness book"— something we can open to find beautiful treasures inside and reminders of what we need to put our attention on to stay happy. We are His children, and He is the one that gives us peace and blessed happiness.

#LevelUpYourFaith

Lord, You are the One who gives us joy and who can turn dark days into days filled with happiness. Today, I will focus on things that are righteous. I will check in with You if I'm feeling down and trust that You will turn my frown upside-down! Thank You for Your grace. In Jesus' name I pray, amen.

#GoGetThemBlessings

You guessed it! I want you to make a happiness box. Write some of your favorite Bible verses on index cards, and on the opposite sides, write why you like the verses. Put them in any kind of box you like, and pull them out when you feel upset, sad, or angry.

> Therefore, if anyone is in Christ, he is a new creation, old things
> have passed away; behold, all things have become new.
> **2 CORINTHIANS 5:17** NKJV

In the animated film *Spider-Man: Into the Spider-Verse*, fictional superhero Miles Morales is at the edge of a building about to take a leap of faith. He had received power like Spider-Man, and he was destined to become the new Spider-Man, but he had to trust what was now inside him. When he jumped, his new self was revealed. The danger and panic of falling quickly to the ground changed into a joyful moment as webs flew out of his palms, and he swung from building to building. His new journey had begun. He was now the new Spider-Man.

For every hero in a comic book, when they find their new power for the first time, it's awkward and difficult to adjust to. *Do I really want this much power?* But like the legendary Stan Lee said, "With great power comes great responsibility." (Believe it or not, this concept is actually from the Bible! Check out Luke 12:48. Maybe even read the entire parable if you want to know more.)

As believers in Christ, we have the power of the Lord at work within us. We just need to believe in it and trust Him to show us how to use that power. It may be awkward and unwieldy at times, but you've been given a divine responsibility. And just like Miles, who leaped and trusted what was now inside him, you'll have to take a leap of faith and trust in the Lord with all your heart if you want to enter into the new life He has for you.

You can trust that God's supernatural, divine power will work in your life. This isn't a comic book. It's real! You might not start swinging from building to building and crime-fighting on the side, but trust me when I say that the Lord will do *far more* than that, far more than you can ask or imagine according to His power at work within you (Ephesians 3:20).

So take that leap!

Lord, thank You for giving me power today and for making me a new creation. I will let go of past hurt, past pain, and all negative thoughts. I will press forward with endurance and strength. You said that I am a conqueror, and I believe it! Thank You, Lord. In Jesus' name I pray, amen.

#GoGetThemBlessings

I want you to put on a fast-paced Christian song of your choice and leap up and down for the entire song. Praise God. Rejoice and leap for joy!

SAFE WITH GOD

The thief does not come except to steal, and to kill, and to destroy. I have come that they may have life, and that they may have *it* more abundantly."
JOHN 10:10 NKJV

#BlessedMode

These days a breaking news report can sound like this: "Thieves are stealing iPhones, taking people's identities, and clearing out their accounts with a fake app. When victims download the app or click on it, it gives their phone a virus, and the thieves now have access to everything in their phone."

But imagine if you heard this on the news: "This just in. Be on the lookout. There is a demon on the loose, a thief coming only to kill, steal, and destroy, and his name is the devil." That would definitely be shocking to hear. But you know what is even more shocking? Both news stories are true! And just like thieves know how your cell phone works, the devil knows how your soul works. He knows how to get inside people's minds and corrupt their souls—if they do not have the right protection.

Think of it like this: we are like God's smartphones. He designed us all to work a certain way. But when we give the devil access into our lives, we download a virus that slowly tries to destroy us, use the information against us, and take total control.

Once we identify the Enemy—the devil!—we need to do a factory reset. Now, on your phone, you back up the things that you see are clean from viruses, right? And when you do a factory reset, it will restore the phone to the way it was originally designed to work, and it will also delete the pesky virus.

But how do you hit the factory reset button on your spiritual life? Repent, and change your perspective. Forgive others and yourself and submit to God's will in your life. Then team up with Jesus and realize that the victory is yours when you follow Him, because the Enemy is already defeated. Jesus is the antivirus, the virus protection we all need. Be alert and pray in the Spirit at all times and on all occasions (Ephesians 6:18).

#LevelUpYourFaith

Lord, today I am strong in You and in Your mighty power. I understand that there is spiritual warfare going on, so I team up with You, Jesus, shouting out "Team Jesus!" and praising Your holy name. I will resist the devil and his schemes. I will be alert and pray persistently. Thank You for Your continuous protection. In Jesus' name I pray, amen.

#GoGetThemBlessings

Take a picture of today's Bible verse, John 10:10, and make it your lock-screen image on your cell phone. Every time you go to pick up your phone, you will be reminded to stay spiritually alert and trust in the Lord.

40

All of us like sheep have gone astray, we have turned, each one, to his own way; but the Lord has caused the wickedness of us all [our sin, our injustice, our wrongdoing] to fall on Him [instead of us].
ISAIAH 53:6 AMP

TAKE TWO . . . OR TWELVE

#BlessedMode

A *take* is a scene recorded in a film or television show. A crew member comes out with a clapper board to synchronize the sound with the picture, saying, "Take one." Then the director yells, "Action!" If the director gets everything he or she needs in that take, it's a celebration for the whole crew because everything was done perfectly.

Most directors like to get a few more takes so they have options to choose from when the footage is being edited. But sometimes they have to redo a take because of a mistake. These "retakes" are done if the sound doesn't record properly, a camera loses power, or an actor messes up a line or misses their mark. A *mark* is where the actor is supposed to stand so the camera can see them perfectly. No matter what they're doing in the scene, as long as they hit the mark, they'll be in focus.

Good directors don't have to do too many retakes because they've prepared for the scene. The actors just need to follow the director's instructions during rehearsal so they're prepared on shoot day. But mistakes happen. Sometimes we have to do retake after retake. You see the finished product, but sometimes we do *hundreds* of takes because of mistakes. And we retake it until we get it right.

Have you ever felt that way in life? Like you're doing the same thing over and over because you missed the mark? You know what

94

you are supposed to do, but when it's time to take action, somehow you lose focus (kind of like the sheep going astray in today's verse). But thank God, because of His grace, we can do a retake and get it right.

Actors rehearse and do run-throughs to prepare for shoot day. When the director yells, "Action!" they know exactly what to do. They also run lines on set and off set. That's what we need to do as believers: prepare and practice. Meditate day and night on the Word, get help from others, and listen to God. Then when your heavenly Father calls "Action!" you're prepared to take direction and you don't miss the mark.

#LevelUpYourFaith

I understand that righteousness comes through faith, Lord. I want to be ready for whatever You want me to do. I will train my mind and spirit to focus on You, hearing Your Word and doing what it says. In Jesus' name I pray, amen.

#GoGetThemBlessings

Memorize a favorite Bible verse. Then grab your phone and record yourself reciting it. See if you can get it in one take. It's okay if you have to do a retake! You'll get better each time.

41

So whatever you wish that others would do to you, do also to them.
MATTHEW 7:12 ESV

SHOPPING CART KINDNESS

#BlessedMode

When I'm done shopping, I always try to return the shopping cart. I just feel like it's the right thing to do. The other day, I watched a shopping-cart attendant clean off some carts for people going into the store. He warmly welcomed the customers when giving them a cart. Not much later, some of those same people walked out of the store, emptied their carts into their cars, and drove off without returning the carts or putting them in the cart corrals. Shopping carts were scattered all over the parking lot, some even blocking parking spaces, but this attendant didn't complain. As he went around the parking lot collecting carts, I realized his actions were a great example of the Golden Rule (which is today's verse).

When you do something for someone and they don't say thank you or show gratitude, it kind of stinks, right? But that doesn't mean you stop being kind or giving off positive, righteous vibes. A few bad apples can throw off your emotions, but don't allow them to derail your consistency. God shows us how to deal with our emotions when our kindness isn't returned:

> Love is patient and kind; love does not envy or boast; it is not arrogant or rude. It does not insist on its own way; it is not irritable or resentful; it does not rejoice at wrongdoing, but rejoices with the truth. Love bears all things, believes all things, hopes all things, endures all things. (1 Corinthians 13:4–7 ESV)

I rely on these verses when I want to go off on someone or when I feel humiliated because I was being kind but got treated badly. I've learned that we don't have to dwell on the negative; we can let it go and move on. And although you may experience a lack of kindness, you can continue to consistently be kind to others. We reap what we sow, and we reap so much more by staying positive, finding gratitude in every moment, and being kind and considerate no matter what.

#LevelUpYourFaith

Lord, I will continue to have a thankful heart, to rejoice always, to pray continually, and to give thanks in all circumstances. Thank You for all You have done and are doing in my life. Just like the one leper out of ten who were cleansed by Jesus, I will always come back to thank You (Luke 17:15). In Jesus' name I pray, amen.

#GoGetThemBlessings

Return your shopping cart the next time you're at a store! Maybe even offer to return someone else's. Say thank you to the cart attendant. Show kindness.

42

UPGRADED

For it is God who works in you to will and to act in order to fulfill his good purpose.
PHILIPPIANS 2:13

#BlessedMode

As Christians, we have been spiritually upgraded. Just like electronics get add-ons when upgraded, when we become new creatures in Christ, we get all kinds of awesome spiritual add-ons—knowledge, gifts, power, purpose, and so much more. And boy, do we have work to do! Now that Jesus is in us, we have godly purpose we've never had before.

God has custom-made and designed each of us, and when we follow Him completely, we are fulfilling His purpose and He is glorified. As new, upgraded creatures, we think differently and act differently. We get new confidence, a new body, and a new mind. The Holy Spirit is inside us now, and He's glowing all over!

But as you probably know, the devil doesn't like the new version of us and will try to interfere—by throwing distractions our way and connecting our past back to us. But because of our new upgrade, given to us from the Lord, old connections and old software just won't connect like they used to anymore. They don't work! It's like when you get a new smartphone and you can't use the old software for your new phone: "This software is not compatible with your upgrade." Well, guess what? *Your past is not compatible with your spiritual upgrade!* I can't imagine a better alert to get. You are new! The past is no longer compatible!

Because Christ is in you, you are better than you were before. Your enemies will take note. "*Whoa!* They came back better, faster, and spiritually stronger. I think we might be in trouble." Your future is so bright and God can now use you for a far greater good and for the bigger-than-life plan he has for you. So let's get upgraded!

#LevelUpYourFaith

Lord, I will accomplish all that I was born to do through Your power. I am a believer, not a doubter! I trust the plans You have for my life and that You will help me. I will work for You, Lord, and I will inspire others to follow You and be blessed by You. In Jesus' name I pray, amen.

#GoGetThemBlessings

Maybe God has been telling you to make a move and do that new thing that He put in your heart, like taking a new job or moving to a new city. Only you know what He has been speaking to you, but today is the day. Toss the anxiety aside and trust in Him. Don't think about past mistakes; just trust the new plan He has given you. If it's from the Lord and you feel it in your heart, like Nike says, "Just do it!"

43

"Be still, and know that I am God."
PSALM 46:10

STOP CHASING

I watched a dog in a yard one day. Every time a person or a car passed by, that dog ran after it, ripping up and down the fence line and barking like crazy, but the fence kept that dog inside the yard, safe with its owner. Eventually, the dog would snap back to reality, look around at its water bowl and bed, and relax in the cool grass. Not even a few minutes later, another car or person would pass by, and the dog start again, barking and pacing up and down the fence. But then it would remember again that it had and everything it needed and would settle down.

I sometimes feel like my attention span is about as long as that dog's. I go running off after some shiny new thing only thirty seconds after God has reminded me of the safety and security I have with Him. He gently reminds me to be still, to stop chasing, that I'm safe and loved with Him (even if I forget again thirty seconds later).

God is telling you today to quiet your spirit and stay close to Him. He has put up His fences of protection to keep you in His peace. What are some of those fences? Time in church, reading the Bible and devotionals, listening to sermons or uplifting podcasts, and spending time with other believers keeps us focused on God's love instead of on the world around us. Unexpected distractions will come that will try to get your attention and pull you away from the love and peace of God. But don't lose focus or forget who you belong to. You belong to God! You can rest in knowing that His love and protection are always with you and will comfort when disaster strikes.

We don't have to be like that forgetful dog, chasing every distraction and emotion thrown at us, reacting with anxiety, anger, jealousy, or fear. Although we don't have a physical fence to keep us from heading down the wrong path, we can choose how we react to distractions, to negativity, to temptation. We can be still and trust God with our next move. We can rest in the cool grass and know that He is in control through the power of His Son, Jesus.

#LevelUpYourFaith

Lord, You made today. You know what is best for me, and I rejoice in the truth that, no matter what happens today, I can rest in Your promise of peace. When I quiet my heart, I can know You. You have given me a clear mind, and You love me. In Jesus' name I pray, amen.

#GoGetThemBlessings

Find some time today to just be still and open your heart to the Lord. A good target is thirty minutes. Find a comfortable place to lie down. Play some worship music and focus on the Lord's presence. Invite the Holy Spirit to comfort and speak to you. If negative thoughts come, imagine that fence of protection guarding you and your mind. Surrender to Jesus and believe that He is working in you.

YOU BELONG

#BlessedMode

We can't control everything that happens in life. The pandemic that started in 2020 sure showed us that, huh? Honestly, it seems like we can't actually control much at all, even with all our education, wisdom, and best intentions.

For me, the pandemic was a huge reminder that new situations will come up in life that will truly shock us, and if we try to control them by ourselves, the stress could really break us down. On some days, I still can't believe everything that has happened in the last couple years.

But I say this all the time, and it's truer than it's ever been: when we team up with Team Jesus, we have security. Jesus is our security! He's our offensive line against the opposing team that follows Satan. Like a football receiver who receives the ball, we receive the truth, salvation, and righteousness through our faith. We are to hold on to them tightly while moving forward through life. And as you persevere, God has an offensive line of grace blocking all defense attacks from the Enemy. The Enemy can make a lot of plays, but he cannot tackle you or take you out.

So don't give up hope if you run into a setback. Stay close to God, learn from it, and keep pushing! Getting proper knowledge and wisdom will help you reach the touchdown every time. The victory is yours, says the Lord (1 Corinthians 15:57). You belong to God, so keep your peace, race with endurance, stay alert, and trust your offensive line of grace, which is making blessed passageways for you to run through.

You belong to God!

My entire life belongs to You, Lord. Everything I have been given in this world is Yours. You are greater than Satan and his attacks. You have overcome the world. Without any doubt, I will push forward, trusting, learning, and growing more spiritually. Today is a blessed day. I will rejoice and be glad in it! In Jesus' name I pray, amen.

#GoGetThemBlessings

Grab a football and a Sharpie. Then mark up the football with positive words about yourself or things that make you feel happy. Once the football is marked up, throw it in the air and catch it. Every time you receive the ball, think about those things you wrote and remember that they are always with you! Keep your joy.

45

GOD'S FIREWORK

They said to each other, "Did not our hearts burn within us while he talked to us on the road, while he opened to us the Scriptures?"
LUKE 24:32 ESV

I love going to watch fireworks with the family during the summer. It's inspiring to see the way the fireworks light up the sky, commanding the attention of everyone at the event. People can't help it with the *ooohhs* and *ahhhs* as blasts and starbursts of light pop in the sky. The bright, shimmering lights illuminate everyone's faces as we gaze at the beautiful display in the sky.

I don't care how old you are, seeing fireworks always induces awe, joy, laughter, and excitement in a crowd. No matter what happened that day or where you come from in the world, when you're watching a fireworks display, something special happens. It's almost like we feel smaller and yet also aware of something bigger and grander—and we're somehow connected as we experience this together.

At the last fireworks show I went to, I was feeling all of these things and couldn't help thinking about how the Holy Spirit does the same thing to our hearts when He fuels us with God's love. Luke's gospel says the disciples' hearts were burning from their encounter with God. His Word breathes a fire in us that ignites a light that explodes and shines on others when we walk into a room. We change the atmosphere because the peace of God is in us. People smile as His goodness shines on them through us, like the bright light of a firework that illuminates a spectator's face.

Your life in Christ is like a Holy Spirit firework! You light up the sky. You make people feel closer to something meaningful.

You can bring people together in new ways. And every day as one of God's children is truly a celebration.

Let's be fireworks for God today! Let's light up the night with praise!

#LevelUpYourFaith

I praise You, Lord! I celebrate Your holy name today. I praise You for your acts of power, for Your surpassing greatness. I thank You for every breath I receive, and with each breath, I give You praise! Thank You, Lord. In Jesus' name I pray, amen.

#GoGetThemBlessings

Buy or make a cupcake or dessert of your choice, and put a candle in it. Then at the end of the day, light the candle and celebrate the day you had. Thank God for a blessed day where you were able to breathe freely and to see another day. Thank Him for all He has done and is doing in your life, and then blow out the candle and eat the dessert! This is a reminder to celebrate every day that you are alive because it is a gift.

46

THE BEST FRAGRANCE

But thank God! He has made us his captives and continues to lead us along in Christ's triumphal procession. Now he uses us to spread the knowledge of Christ everywhere, like a sweet perfume. Our lives are a Christ-like fragrance rising up to God. But this fragrance is perceived differently by those who are being saved and by those who are perishing.

2 CORINTHIANS 2:14–15 NLT

#BlessedMode

I like to wear cologne. Smelling good is a priority for me when grooming. I also love it when cologne companies offer lotion, shampoo, and bodywash with the same fragrance as their signature cologne. This enhances the aroma. The scents I continue to restock are the ones my Asia loves; she is the closest to me and will smell it every day. Another thing that makes me repurchase a cologne is when people say, "What cologne are you wearing? That smells great." And, of course, it has to smell pleasant to me when I rub it on my skin, because it is on me and I smell it everywhere I go. If it is a strong enough fragrance, people can smell it before I even walk into the room.

Cologne doesn't work until you apply it on your skin. Lotion doesn't work until you rub it in. I know because it has become part of my daily routine.

It's the same with God: the more you apply God into your life—His love, His will—His presence will rub off on you and His desires will become your desires. Your decisions will change, your thoughts will change, because He is now on you and with you. And as you prosper in the knowledge of God, the people who are paying close attention or who get a whiff of your spiritual

106

success will ask, "What have you been doing?" Then you let them know about the God you serve, and when you do that, you are spreading the knowledge of Christ everywhere you go. Like a sweet fragrance.

#LevelUpYourFaith

I want to smell sweet in Your presence, Lord! I will apply Your wisdom to every aspect of my life. Where I go, You go too. In Jesus' name I pray, amen.

#GoGetThemBlessings

Go try some colognes or perfumes at a fragrance store. Ask questions and find a new fragrance that you like. It's a fun experience to learn more about fragrances. As you do this, think about how God sought you out, found you, and saved you.

47

WE LIVE THIS

Therefore go and make disciples of all nations, baptizing them in the name of the Father and of the Son and of the Holy Spirit, and teaching them to obey everything I have commanded you. And surely I am with you always, to the very end of the age."
MATTHEW 28:19–20

#BlessedMode

I was drinking out of my shaker bottle from MusclePharm the other day when I noticed the words, "We live this!" on the side of the bottle. I thought to myself, *That is a really cool statement and model.* It reminds me that I'm making a healthy lifestyle part of my life—not just something I do for one day or a season, but for life. It's part of who I am now. I live it. It is a confidence builder. It reminds me to keep pushing, keep working, and never stop grinding!

And the "We" on my shaker bottle is also saying to me there are others like me who are conquering obstacles, remaining dedicated, and wanting to see the dreams they have envisioned become a reality. Once you "live it," no one can take it away from you. No one can steal your joy or your zeal because you have passion for the life you are living!

We as believers can say "We live this" as we build our resilience, keep pressing toward the goal, and continue using our faith. We *live it*—our faith—every day. And this is so much more than a gym session. The Holy Spirit is in us! We have confident assurance and freedom from doubt. We have spiritual eyes that are wide open and clarity on His purpose for us. Jesus is God in the flesh, our Redeemer, sent by God to save us from sin so we can live in His truth forever. And we can know the truth more and more as we study, train, learn, and grow spiritually.

When you're saved, you become a student of Jesus just like His disciples were. That's right—*we are also disciples*. Once we give our life to Christ and follow Him, we are supposed to spread the gospel to others, making more disciples. *We live this!* And here is what is so beautiful about all this: the "we" includes *Jesus*. He is with us as we minister, testify, sing His praises, forgive others, and stay faithful: "And surely I am with you always, to the very end of the age" (Matthew 28:20). He is with you always and forever as you disciple with and for Him.

Rejoice today! We are one with Christ and all believers. *We live this!*

#LevelUpYourFaith

Lord, I am a true worshiper. I will continue to worship Your holy name in Spirit and in truth! I will continue to tell others about Your love, Your power, and Your grace, which You give freely to believers. In Jesus' name I pray, amen.

#GoGetThemBlessings

Grab a bottle that can hold a gallon of water. Take this bottle of water with you everywhere you go today with the mission to finish it—but it is okay if you don't. I want you to see how far you can get and to know that with every sip you are doing something good for your body. Think of how the Word of God cleanses and hydrates your spirit as you also cleanse and hydrate your body. It feels good.

48

In their hearts humans plan their course, but the Lord establishes their steps.
PROVERBS 16:9

HOLY TO-DO LIST

#BlessedMode

Have you ever been in prayer and God gives you an assignment or a to-do list? When He does that, move on it at that moment. You have to be ready to move when God tells you to move, so you can be at the right destination at the right time. Do what God tells you to do. He establishes your steps.

You want answered prayer? You have to move in His timing! It's like this: you are at the crosswalk of life, where the sign says to walk, but you don't do it. Now you have to sit there and wait, and you're going to be late to your destination because you did not pay attention to the sign. Don't be late to your blessing. Walk to your purpose. When God tells you to move, do it then. No thinking about it, no distractions. Move!

Don't get stuck wondering while you're waiting. Sometimes answered prayers are hiding in the sacrifices you need to make in your life or the discipline you need to build in your life. I've learned some of these lessons the hard way. When I haven't moved when God has told me to, things have gotten pushed back. Obstacles have come up. My goals have been further away because I stayed on the sidelines. But I eventually learned. I listened more closely when God said to move. And when He said, "Go!" I moved without fear, even when it seemed scary and crazy. And when the blessings came, I understood—because they were often far more than I would have imagined.

You can experience this too. I want you to know what it feels like to move . . . and then see why God said to in the first place. Prepare to have your socks knocked off and to say, "Wow, God. So *this* is why You said to move!" I promise that He's ready to do more than you could ever imagine.

49

A RESET

And after you have suffered a little while, the God of all grace, who has called you to his eternal glory in Christ, will himself restore, confirm, strengthen, and establish you.
1 PETER 5:10 ESV

#BlessedMode

A message will pop up in video games when something has stopped gameplay: "Reset or Game over?" Perhaps it's an obstacle you can't defeat. *Reset* will start the game again *on the same level*. That's a good thing! Because you know that level and you get better with each try. Eventually you'll beat it. But if you hit *game over*, you wipe out the whole game and start a new one. That really stinks depending on how many levels you've already defeated.

Hitting *reset* is the best option. You know what to look for, what tripped you up, and you're ready to conquer. So you hit *reset* until you get it right. And when you finish that level, the joy is out of this world.

In life, you can also reach a level or obstacle that sets you back. It can feel overwhelming, like you're being asked the same question: "Reset or Game over?" Whatever you do, don't hit the "power off" button! That's what some people do when the emotional toll and the stress get to be too much. They give up on life or try to forget their troubles by falling into harmful habits. Or they just remain in a stuck place, believing that nothing can change.

Just like when you hit *reset* in a video game, the Holy Spirit knows what you've been through and where you need to go. You don't have to start from the beginning. He knows when you need to go to God and say, "I can't handle this, Lord. I need Your help.

Take this burden away from me, please, and set things anew in my life." That's when He reminds you of the victory that was already won on the cross when Jesus saved you from sin.

You have the assurance of salvation! God will renew your zeal to push forward, and He will continue to refresh your spirit. So hit *reset* and get to work with God! You know what's coming. You know the obstacle that knocked you down. Snap out of those thoughts of defeat, and *go get them blessings*.

#LevelUpYourFaith

You placed the Holy Spirit within me to be a constant help. I know that when I go to You in prayer, my prayers are heard and that You, Lord, will make all things new. In Jesus' name I pray, amen.

#GoGetThemBlessings

Find a small wastebasket and five pieces of paper. On each piece of paper, write down something you need to stop doing (being angry, unforgiving, or jealous for example). Then crumple each piece of paper, and play some good ol' trash can basketball. If you don't get them in on the first try, reset and try again.

Whoever desires to love life and see good days, let him keep
his tongue from evil and his lips from speaking deceit.
1 PETER 3:10 ESV

#BlessedMode

Your words shape your reality. If you speak with warm, kind
words, it sets a tone and others are likely to respond in a similar
fashion. If you speak negatively, you can bring people, including
yourself, down real fast. Have you ever been around someone who
is just negative in their speech? They assume a horrible outcome.
They believe the worst of the world. They can't seem to see a good
thing anywhere—and their speech reflects it. It can really make
you feel awful, huh?

Your speech has power! Don't speak the opposite of what
you've prayed about. For all the things you've prayed about pri-
vately regarding a situation, make sure your speech publicly (if
it's something you'd talk about) reflects the spirit in which you
prayed. If you make positive confessions during prayer time, keep
them when you speak to others. Don't let the distractions of the
day cause you to speak against what you confirmed in prayer.
Sometimes when I'm stressed, I can go into a negative mindset
that is reflected in my words. But that doesn't match my heart or
my prayers for the day! So I work actively to be mindful and aware
at all times—and to "speak" the heart of my prayers in word and
deed. The same is true for anything positive you're praying for.
Whatever blessing you want to see manifested in your life? Speak
it out loud. Don't just agree with someone's perspective if it doesn't
line up with the answer God has given you.

Your righteous speech will make known to everyone the God

you serve and that it is *His truth* you are standing on. You won't be moved because your faith is strong. Blessings will come to pass and all who witness will be moved by God's grace and kindness in your life. They will be inspired by your testimony, and they may begin to see how they can align their prayers and their words to show God's power in their lives.

Let's put some positive goodness in the atmosphere! As you pray it, also say it—so the world can see God's goodness and power at all times.

#LevelUpYourFaith

Lord, guard my lips. Help me not be so pushed or pressured by the stress of life that I blurt out evil. I want my words to be gracious, positive, and uplifting. Let my words be Your words and my speech always be pleasing to Your ear. In Jesus' name I pray, amen.

#GoGetThemBlessings

Write down positive words and actions about how you want to act or feel today. For example, "I am smart, I am strong, I am beautiful, and I am wise." Say these words out loud over and over again. As your ears hear you say them, your body will absorb these truths as well. Trust me! You will feel empowered.

> Remember not the former things, nor consider the things of old. Behold, I am doing a new thing; now it springs forth, do you not perceive it? I will make a way in the wilderness and rivers in the desert."
> ISAIAH 43:18–19 ESV

THROWBACK THURSDAY

#BlessedMode

On Thursdays, people often post old pictures on social media using the hashtag #TBT (Throwback Thursday). I sometimes get in on the fun and post favorite memories or some entertaining moments from my career. I am here to tell you that #TBT is a fun walk down memory lane, but don't get stuck there! Living in the past keeps you from enjoying the present and working toward the future. Sometimes spending too much time in the past can also be depressing or can pull you back into times when you weren't happy, when you weren't walking in truth, when you weren't seeing God's future for you.

So make new memories! Recognize the good things in your life *today*. What if we added #TCT on Tuesdays? For #TodayCountsTuesday? And we started sharing all the good gifts happening in our lives right this minute? I think we should!

Stop letting people throw you back to your past like that's all you've got, like your best days are behind you. They aren't! God promises us that in His Word! So thank Him for today and get started on something new. Move onward and forward, and become what you've always wanted to become. The best is yet to come!

Some people look on the past with ongoing regret or think that was the best they could do. Sometimes they can't move on from the mistakes they made. Let it go. It's a new day, a new you, a new future! And *God has made you new.* Make new memories and reach for new dreams. Celebrate the #TBT victories, but don't stay a #TBT. *You are not your past!* Shout out the #TBT and then dive into the #TCT . . . because today counts (and tomorrow counts!) and God is ready to show you how.

#LevelUpYourFaith

Help me move forward, Lord. Help me to go after the dreams You have given me in my heart. I look forward to the start of each new day because I know it is a day You have made! Thank You for all the love You give me and my family. In Jesus' name I pray, amen.

#GoGetThemBlessings

Grab a piece of paper and a pencil, and write at the top of the paper, "I am doing a new thing." Then below it, write down one or two past accomplishments. Look at them for a few seconds and thank God for helping you with them. Then write next to each accomplishment a big check mark indicating it is done—you did it. Now write down one or two things you want to accomplish and see manifested in your life. Then write, "Jesus did it before, and He can do it again. New blessings are on the way!"

BYO-BREAKTHROUGH

Sometimes I get asked, "Why are you always happy?" and I respond by saying, "Because God woke me up this morning."

Before I even start my day, I bring all the worry, anxiety, concern, and drama from yesterday and any questions to God *first*. So by the time you see me, I've already had a pep talk with our heavenly Father, prayed, and worked out my body and my spirit. I'm *ready* for the day and protected from anything that the Enemy wants to try and throw at me. I have already determined that no matter what the day brings, I'll keep my peace, and I will keep my family protected.

Author and evangelist Cindy Trimm says, "The possibilities in your life change when your perspective changes." That is so true! If you're looking through the eyes of Christ, you see the possibilities He sees for your life. Proverbs 29:18 says it best: "If people can't see what God is doing, they stumble all over themselves; but when they attend to what he reveals, they are most blessed" (MSG). I attend to what God reveals when I spend time with Him every day in prayer.

Look, every day should be a praise party for us because God has woken us up again to triumph in a new day. We should always remain joyful. It's a party! And since it is a party, remember to BYOB: "bring your own breakthrough." I got that quote from Pastor Steven Furtick of Elevation Church, and it is very powerful. I'm sure you were shocked to see the acronym BYOB in a devotional, but we are not talking about beer; we are talking about breakthroughs! Wake up expecting a breakthrough in your life, knocking down barriers. Today is the day to do better than the day before. God has your back! Go get them blessings! It's a praise party!

I will rejoice! I will praise Your holy name! I expect breakthroughs every day. I expect victories every day. Following You, Lord, brings both victories and breakthroughs. In Jesus' name I pray, amen.

#GoGetThemBlessings

My sensei back in the day in Chicago was Bishop Frank Holbrook, who taught us kung fu and tae kwon do. He was also one of the deacons at my church, and he would have us learn "katas," or choreographed moves, while reciting Bible verses. I want you to kick—yep, kick! If you do not have the ability to kick, then punch. With every kick or punch, imagine that you are breaking through obstacles in your life. Start off by saying, "This is the day (punch or kick) the Lord has made (punch or kick). Let us rejoice (punch or kick) and be glad in it (punch or kick)." Remember God gives us the strength to power through our day, to keep our joy while we fight, and to destroy obstacles in our way. Do this as many times as you want, learning not to fight with anger but with the joy and love of the Lord. Keep pushing and growing!

53

I can do all this through him who gives me strength.
PHILIPPIANS 4:13

DON'T GIVE UP

A friend of mine posted a video on social media of a kid skateboarding, trying to get a trick right. He was trying to grind down a rail, and he kept falling off the skateboard. But he kept trying. And on the twentieth try, he nailed it!

Then I saw another video of a kid at a gymnastics tournament, and he and the other students were in a line, doing flips one after another. Finally, it was his turn and he couldn't do it. He kept trying, but he still couldn't do it. Some people in the crowd yelled out, "It's okay. You can stop!"

But that kid *kept pushing*. It was such a moving moment when everyone started to encourage him. It took a long time, but he finally did it. The crowd screamed and jumped out of their seats, celebrating him and his accomplishment. And his family cried tears of joy. His friends ran up to hug him. Talk about perseverance!

My message for you today is: Don't give up.

Never give up. You are almost there. It might feel like you're nowhere close to where you're trying to go, but I promise that God is with you and taking you there. Keep going. If you fall down twenty times, get back up twenty-one times. Envision the victory moment before you get to it. Have faith. Hold on to your determination.

God makes so many promises to us in the Bible, and they're all true. Every last one of them. And He says *you can do all things through Christ*. All things. Even that thing that keeps tripping you up or seems impossible. You can do it.

So don't give up. You are almost to victory!

#LevelUpYourFaith

Lord, I want to say thank You! Thank You for the endurance, thank You for the strength, and thank You for the wisdom to get things done. Thank You for goals achieved and for spiritual breakthroughs. Thank You for always helping me. In Jesus' name I pray, amen.

#GoGetThemBlessings

You may be tired and discouraged, but there's a difference between taking a break and quitting. Today, take a moment to pause and silence your mind of noise or any negative self-talk. Just sit in the quiet and meditate on the scripture for today: "I can do all this through Him who gives me strength." Let this verse inspire you and remind you of the good work you're doing—and to keep going!

54

F.R.O.G.

#BlessedMode

Fully Rely On God. F.R.O.G.

Since I fully rely on God, I guess I'm feeling a little froggy today!

Have you ever heard the saying, "If you feel froggy, then leap"? That is usually something you hear right before someone is about to fight. Now, y'all know I love reminding you that we are engaged in spiritual warfare. We need to win the war by following the teachings of Jesus—the winner who has already won the battle.

Here's the thing: the devil knows Jesus has already won. That is why his mission is to confuse us and make us think the battle hasn't been won. He wants us to make it a habit to focus on negative emotions and thoughts, mistakes, tough issues, anything but God so we won't get up and pray and meditate and praise. He tries to knock us down each day, hoping we won't leap up with faith the next time the bell rings.

This bell I'm talking about is a boxing ring bell. Boxing is really all about skill. You have to find the right time to attack, determine your opponent's unguarded weak spots, and hit those parts. Then you hope they give up or throw in the towel. It's the same with faith. Guard your heart and protect your family from the Enemy by trusting in the Lord and fully relying on Him. God will find and protect every unguarded weak spot in your life. Nothing will be exposed for the Enemy to take advantage of or steal from your life. But you must be obedient and consistent in your righteousness. You must ask God for what you need in prayer. And of course, Fully Rely on God. Are you feeling froggy?

#LevelUpYourFaith

I rely on You always, Lord. I believe that if I ask, I will receive. I believe that You will watch over me and my family, always protecting me from my enemies. In Jesus' name I pray, amen.

#GoGetThemBlessings

Download a free boxing round interval timer app or set a timer on your smartphone. Set the time for three-minute intervals: three minutes of exercise and three minutes of rest. Shadow box, jog, or jump rope. Just get physical and do this for twelve rounds of three minutes each. Every time you rest, think about the Lord restoring your energy to get you through the next round.

55

DO GOOD

Let us not become weary in doing good,
for at the proper time we will reap a
harvest if we do not give up.
GALATIANS 6:9

#BlessedMode

Before I became a youth pastor at Spirit Food Christian Center, I worked with our church media team. I was the stage manager, and I would help post content on our social media platforms. One Sunday our pastor, Garry Zeigler, said some uplifting words in his sermon that I knew people would enjoy hearing the next day on our social media platforms. So on Sunday night before bed, I edited a fun recap video with graphics and music and posted it on our social media. The next morning I started my Monday routine that was packed with things to do.

A couple of hours into the day, I got a text from my cousin saying, "Hey, the video you posted . . . is it supposed to *not* have sound?"

I was like, "Wait, is the sound not working?" So I quickly went to the post and found it had some kind of glitch when uploading. The sound was completely gone. I was overwhelmed because I was now busy doing other tasks, but I knew the message in this post would help someone. So I immediately thought to myself, *Faint not in well doing*, and I made time to fix the video. I knew it would help somebody, inspire them, give them encouragement, and put happiness in their heart, so I rearranged my schedule a little to squeeze in some time to do again what God had told me to do.

And He was correct in giving me that desire—because based

on the comments on that post, the words people heard were a blessing to many. Is there something you're facing today where God is asking you to *faint not in well doing*?

#LevelUpYourFaith

I am never too busy to do Your will, God. You always restore my time and energy, and even when I'm tired, You help me to press on and not give up. Thank You, Lord! In Jesus' name I pray, amen.

#GoGetThemBlessings

Set a timer on your phone that gives you a reminder alert every three hours. When you hear the alert, no matter what you are doing, I want you to stop, take a deep breath in and out, and say, "Thank You, Lord. I praise Your holy name." If you are with someone at the moment the alarm goes off, tell them what you are about to do and ask if they want to join in and say it with you. How cool will that be? Now that's Blessed Mode! And if you are up to it, at the end of the day or the next day, post on your social media how this exercise made you feel.

56

Yet in all these things we are more than conquerors through Him who loved us.
ROMANS 8:37 NKJV

#BlessedMode

I love the quote by motivational speaker Tim Storey: "When you have a setback, don't take a step back. God is already preparing your comeback."

I've had some of my own setbacks in life. An interviewer asked one time about the time I contemplated suicide: "Where was God in those moments?" God was there! But I wasn't. Satan was there as well, and I was focusing on the thoughts and feelings Satan was stirring in me instead of on God.

I had been going through a down time and was dealing with a ton of emotions, setbacks, heartache, disappointment, and bad decisions. But I still had hope. I wanted to be saved! But my faith was weak. And the devil latched onto my fear: "The world would be better off without you." Have you ever heard those words? I want you to know something: Satan *knows* the force for God you can be. He knew that about me too and would have loved to stop me!

But God stepped in. He never left my side. He hugged me close. And I felt a reason to live even though I couldn't see a brighter future. God said, "You're still here. And I love you. Just stay close to Me."

God wants you to know that, if you're still here, He will renew your mind. He can light your path in ways that seem impossible. And He will lead you away from the emotions and bad choices that have plagued you. Sometimes we need to be reminded of the strength we have in Jesus. That's why I love to shout out phrases like #TeamJesus!, #AllGod!, and #GoGetThemBlessings! God sees you and knows you. He knit you together in your mother's womb. You are special to Him. And He will pick you up out of the rubble and make you new.

Somebody might have done you wrong or you might've gotten bad news, and the shock of it feels like a hit to the chest—but you will recover. Don't give up! Speak God's greatness into your life. Speak life, not death. Positivity, not negativity. God wants you to learn in this moment so that you will be able to help others with your testimony. Continue to be prayerful and ask God to give you wisdom and strength. Say right now out loud, "I will recover!" Know who you are in Christ Jesus. We are more than conquerors. *It's comeback season!*

#LevelUpYourFaith

My faith is bigger than my fear. My love is bigger than the hate from the Enemy. I will recover because You, Lord, heal all wounds and give me divine strength and healing! In Jesus' name I pray, amen.

#GoGetThemBlessings

Write down "I will recover" and then under it "Romans 8:37." Then tape this simple but effective reminder that *you will make it* in a place where you'll see it every day.

57

EVERY STEP

> The LORD directs the steps of the godly. He delights in every detail of their lives.
> **PSALM 37:23** NLT

No matter where you are in your particular roles, there are always new things to learn and new levels of growth. Before I became a youth pastor at my church, I was the stage manager. I saw a need and decided to help. Before starting, I met with my pastor, Pastor Garry D. Zeigler, to hear his vision for the church. God had given him a ton of ideas. One of them was to have a new order of service.

As I started implementing some of the changes, one step at a time, a few members resisted. Some even threatened to leave the church. I caught myself focusing too much on others' opinions. Asia and I prayed about it. "God told you what to do for Him," she said. "Stay focused on the vision and the plan." Thank God for a praying wife who gets word from the Holy Spirit!

I started to read *The Ministry of Helps Handbook* by Dr. Buddy Bell during my time of worship and prayer, and many of the stories spoke to me. One part broke down the difference between *volunteering* and *helping*. I began to realize that some people didn't understand that they weren't simply volunteers; they were doing ministry, which requires a willing heart. I prayed for our members, that we would all work toward the same vision: "If two of you on earth agree about anything they ask for, it will be done for them by my Father in heaven" (Matthew 18:19 ESV).

And guess what? Hearts began to soften. We worked together.

Don't skip the steps! Because every step is important. Some are difficult and some are easy, but they all get you to the blessings.

We could have gotten stuck on a step when people started to feel fearful or upset. Thank the Lord we didn't.

Bobby Brown sang a song called "Every Little Step." It actually makes me think of God and how He's with me every step of the way! I know Bobby wasn't talking about God, but it still really connects for me. God wants you to know that He is there with you, with every little step you take. He wants you to learn something with every step. And every step is a blessing because it will give you the knowledge to get to the next step, and the next step after that, and so on and on. Blessing to blessing. Let's take the steps together.

#LevelUpYourFaith

Order my steps, Lord! Show me the way I should go. I honor and obey You, Lord. You are awesome, and all my help comes from You. I need Your knowledge today, so teach me, Lord. In Jesus' name I pray, amen.

#GoGetThemBlessings

Take the stairs! Find some stairs and imagine yourself getting to your goal with each step. If you want to take this even further, take the stairs all week. Thank God for each step you climb.

SLOW TO ANGER

understand this, my beloved brothers and sisters. Let
everyone be quick to hear [be a careful, thoughtful listener],
slow to speak [a speaker of carefully chosen words and],
slow to anger [patient, reflective, forgiving].
JAMES 1:19 AMP

#BlessedMode

Anger can be a distraction. Think about the last time you got angry. What did you do? Maybe you thought about it (and kept thinking about it). You told people about it. You forgot about the things you were supposed to be doing instead because you were so focused on this thing that made you angry. God had a purpose for you, but you were stuck thinking about what someone said or did.

For example, you know where you need to be and you know where you need to go, but someone makes you angry. They take you away from what you need to be doing and try to distract you from your blessing. And the next thing you know, you're off track.

Or think about social media comments. You can get fifty good, uplifting comments, but when one person fires off a bogus, negative comment, you get all upset. Don't get angry in the first place! I know it's easier said than done, but someone being hateful on social media isn't worth the energy of anger. Ignore it. Be slow to anger. You don't have time to put all your attention on that negativity. You have things to do; you're on a mission with God!

Instead of getting angry, pray for person who has said or done something hurtful. Softly say, "Lord, I forgive this person, for they know not what they do. I don't know what is going on in their life, but I pray that you will touch their heart and soften it. You have forgiven me for so much, and I thank You." This prayer takes only a few seconds, and beyond praying for God's touch on this person's life, those few seconds will help you as well. Remember that you can do all things through Christ (Philippians 4:13), and that includes learning how to avoid anger.

Anger just isn't worth it. Take a breath and let it go.

#LevelUpYourFaith

I will take time to listen to my heart and Your will when I feel like my emotions are about to ignite in anger. I will choose peace instead of pain. I will take time to think on positive responses, and I will look to You for help as I let go of any unforgiveness in my heart. In Jesus' name I pray, amen.

#GoGetThemBlessings

Think about people who get on your nerves, make you angry, or disrupt your day, and then say softly out loud, "Forgive____, for they know not what they do." This is a way to give the issue or problem to God and keep your joy. Remember, we choose to keep our joy!

59

NO BEEF

#BlessedMode

You may notice something after you invite God into your life. People start to see a change in you and start saying things like, "You're different," "You're so peaceful now," or "What's going on with you?"

God's light in you can be confusing for onlookers. Some people see that light and want to know more because they want it for themselves. But there are also some haters. . . . They see that you're different, and it probably makes them uncomfortable. They may try to bring up your past and how you used to be. They may try and lure you back into sin or push the buttons that used to get you upset, cussing and arguing.

But something crazy happens when the Lord is in you and people push those old buttons—they don't work like they used to! And that can really tick people off. Eventually, they'll probably give up. Why don't the buttons work anymore? Because although you live in the flesh, you are not *of* the flesh. You are God's new creation, holy and filled with His Spirit. You are not about that beef anymore! You are now a "Good Burger," LOL. You don't have time for meatheads. Meatheads only think with the flesh, not the spirit. (And . . . those very meatheads may be the ones who ultimately look to you for the hope you have in Christ, so don't give up on them.)

So no need for beef around here. The battle is already won! Jesus won it! He did this just for you. The victory is already won, so go get them blessings!

#LevelUpYourFaith

I am a winner, not a sinner. Winning is inside me, not envy or jealousy. And I have already won because I am a follower of the One who has the victory, Jesus Christ! Thank You, Lord, for getting me to each goal in my life, for giving me spiritual endurance and divine knowledge. In Jesus' name I pray, amen.

#GoGetThemBlessings

Stand in front of your mirror and practice some boxing moves. Say out loud, "Today I am good. God created me to win. I am a winner in Him!"

"So watch yourselves. 'If your brother
or sister sins against you, rebuke them;
and if they repent, forgive them.'"
LUKE 17:3

EARLIER THAN SATAN

#BlessedMode

The Enemy gets up early planning for our downfall, so as believers we gotta get up *earlier*—to pray for victory and to get proper instruction. This is spiritual warfare, so we must fight with prayer, consistency, and determination, spreading God's love and being an ambassador for Christ!

The character Ryu, in the video game *Street Fighter*, uses a special attack, a wave motion of energy that comes out of his fist like a ball of fire and destroys his enemies. He yells out a war cry, "Hadouken!" I've always thought that sounds a lot like "Rebuke it!" so let's apply that same idea here.

As believers, the way we win this spiritual battle is by rebuking sin and wrongdoing. But what does *rebuke* mean? I bet you aren't using that word in everyday conversation, LOL. It means "sharp disapproval." When the Enemy says your dreams won't come true, pray and say, "I disapprove of that!" When people say you won't make it to your goals, pray and say, "I disapprove of that!" When you feel like you'll never move past disappointment, sweep your arm and say, "I rebuke it!"

Yes, we all have daily battles on earth, but this fight is bigger—it's in the spiritual realm. The amazing thing is that *the battle is already won*. You just need to stay close to the One who has won the battle for you! Jesus will give you hope and power, will point you in the right direction, will teach you what to rebuke and what to support. So pray, meditate on the Word, and praise His holy name. And when the Enemy appears and tries to throw you off course, be ready to rebuke him in Jesus' name!

#LevelUpYourFaith

Lord, You said that victory is mine, and I believe that today. I will not let ungodly people tell me how to live my life. I will always look to You for all my answers. My righteousness is essential. I am intentional about my faith. Your love and wisdom never fail, Lord. In Jesus' name I pray, amen.

#GoGetThemBlessings

When you feel things start to go sideways, remind yourself that God is on your side. All things are working out in your favor. Listen to the song "Intentional" by Travis Greene and meditate on God's love never failing in your life.

61

Finally, brothers and sisters, whatever is true, whatever is noble, whatever is right, whatever is pure, whatever is lovely, whatever is admirable—if anything is excellent or praiseworthy—think about such things.
PHILIPPIANS 4:8

DISTRACTIONS

#BlessedMode

The term *tunnel vision* usually has a negative connotation, but I actually think there are areas in life where it makes sense to have a little tunnel vision . . . some God-inspired tunnel vision.

When you are running in the right direction, when you're making choices and taking actions ordained by God, haters often try to get your attention, to distract you, to lure you off the path God has for you. Sometimes when they see you living in the fullness of God's blessings, they're even *more* motivated to get you going in the wrong direction. And once they've distracted you and discouraged you and even got you on the *path* toward the wrong direction, these naysayers have already drained your energy.

One day a while back, someone sent me a bunch of negative texts that really threw me off my game. I knew I shouldn't respond or engage, but the temptation to defend myself or prove a point got the best of me, and I typed my way right into a text war with this person. And it went on for an hour! Try to guess what that text war accomplished. Yep—a whole lotta nothing. In addition, it had distracted me from what I needed to be doing and had thrown off my entire day. I felt like God was telling me, "I gave you an out, Kel! You *knew* you shouldn't have engaged . . . but you did it anyway. I stopped to meditate and pray, and God reminded me the enemy loves to distract when we're on a mission for God.

Next time you encounter a person or activity or conversation that you can see isn't from the Lord and is going to take you off task, walk away from it in Jesus' name. Do not get distracted! Focus on the lovely, the pure, the holy . . . the work God has for you as you share His blessings with the world. Lock your eyes and your heart on God, on things that are positive, and on people who are on a mission with you.

#LevelUpYourFaith

Lord, help me to keep my focus. Distractions arise and are so easy to grab on to. When distractions come, help me not to follow them. Your Word is true; Your words are kind; the guidance You give my spirit is a blessing. And I will follow You and the things You want for me always. In Jesus' name I pray, amen.

#GoGetThemBlessings

Take several deep breaths in and out. Relax and quiet your mind, and when you are ready, reread Philippians 4:8 slowly. Proclaim out loud, "I think on these things."

62

If one gives an answer before he hears, it is his folly and shame.
PROVERBS 18:13 ESV

LISTEN CLOSELY

#BlessedMode

Have you ever had someone listen to you? I mean like *really* listen and understand and totally get you? I know I have, and that has made all the difference in areas of my life where I felt misunderstood or just really needed someone to hear and see the real me.

We all need someone to listen closely, so let's work on being that someone for others.

- **Take time to listen.** When you're in a conversation with someone, slow down. Take time to actually *really* listen and hear what they are saying.
- **Be attentive.** Even if you disagree or have thoughts or feedback, stop and pay attention. Don't sit there thinking about what you want to say next. Listen. Then form your thoughts. Sometimes we start formulating our response because we think we're right. And maybe you are! But let the other person speak before deciding that.
- **Listen to learn.** Listening helps you learn more about a person. You might start to realize that what they're saying makes sense (or maybe it doesn't make sense at all and you can explain to them why later). Relax and listen to them to learn the whole story.

Ultimately, you might end the conversation agreeing to disagree or walking away with both of you getting a proper understanding of each other's true feelings. Here's an important truth: listening and responding without anger and without rushing creates a healthy atmosphere for conversation and for truth to be revealed and understanding gained. And isn't that what we all want?

#LevelUpYourFaith

Lord, help me to listen and be attentive. Help me to be in the moment and actually present in conversations with family members, significant others, and friends. That way I can respond in an honest and loving way. In Jesus' name I pray, amen.

#GoGetThemBlessings

Try listening today. Before you have a conversation, ask the person how they're doing and listen to their response before you talk about yourself or your day. If you're alone today, call a friend or family member, ask them about their day. Listen and be attentive to what they say.

63

A merry heart makes a cheerful countenance,
But by sorrow of the heart the spirit is broken.
PROVERBS 15:13 NKJV

A MERRY HEART

Sometimes we are surprised to find out someone has been going through a deep depression because it seemed like they had it all together. A lot of us are going through silent struggles or are good at keeping our difficulties to ourselves. You truly never know what someone else is going through unless you ask.

When a heart is filled with sorrow or someone's spirit is broken, that's exactly when intentional kindness is needed. When I went through a serious bout of depression—staring suicide in the face—a simple and unprovoked check-in from people who cared made all the difference. Knowing that I was loved, that someone was thinking about me, was a key part of bringing me out of my despair.

There's a lot going on in the world right now, and so many people are struggling in ways we can't even comprehend. That's why it's so important for us to spread love as much as possible. We have so much power to share God's love with the world and with hurting hearts!

You can change a person's entire day by simply letting them know that you love them. You can give them a boost, brighten their spirit, and offer hope. Give someone a call and say, "I don't need anything. I just wanted to let you know I love you." It will feel so good for them—and for you!

Spread love, not hate. You know that saying "Give me my flowers now, not when I'm gone"? Let someone know that you appreciate them and that they are loved *today*. Knowing that you are loved and seen can help a person come out of whatever dark times they are in. So show love and put a big smile on some faces today! I guarantee it will put a big smile on yours as well.

#LevelUpYourFaith

The joy You give me, Lord, is so important. Help me share it with others so they can feel Your peace. Help them to be happy and not worried, to be cheerful and not sorrowful. Turn every frown upside down today, Lord! In Jesus' name I pray, amen.

#GoGetThemBlessings

Tell three people today that you love them, and ask if you can pray for them. Let the Lord guide your words.

64

NOT FOR YOU

#BlessedMode

When in doubt . . . don't! If you know a choice or action is wrong or if there's a ton of confusion surrounding it, then you shouldn't do it. The Holy Spirit is saying, "Naw, this is not for you."

I had a situation when I was a kid where two kids in my neighborhood wanted me to do something illegal. But I knew it was wrong and would land me in trouble, so I walked away. An hour later I saw a squad car going through the neighborhood, and those kids were in the back of it. I was so thankful I hadn't made the same choice! Don't get pressured into the wrong choices. Take control of your future.

Around that time, my parents had me in the church every Sunday. Now, I'm not saying I always made the right decisions as a kid because I attended church on Sundays, but the Lord was with me, and I was in His presence regularly. My parents put positivity around me and showed me what faith was, and the prayers of my family and my church family protected me and opened the door to God working in my life. Those prayers are still working now.

Pastor Steven Furtick once said, "You can control your choices but not the consequences from those choices." This is so true! So make sure your choices are righteous and of God. And if you are a parent reading this, continue to keep your kids covered in prayer. Prayer truly works!

Heavenly Father, thank You for being with me when I have difficult decisions to make. Continue to open my ears and my heart to pay attention to Your guidance. Lead me on the path of life. In Jesus' name I pray, amen.

#GoGetThemBlessings

Prayer does work! Take some time and meditate on this quote: "Let your faith roar so loud that you can't hear what doubt is saying." This week, I want you to try a "fixed-hour prayer" and stick with it. For example, pray at 7:00 o'clock every morning (or whatever time of the day you choose), and make it the same every day. This is awesome to do because it structures your day around your prayers, not the other way around. You will be making God the center of each day and developing a meaningful habit in the process.

65

Whatever you have learned or received or heard from me, or seen in me—put it into practice. And the God of peace will be with you.

PHILIPPIANS 4:9

LEARN FROM MISTAKES

#BlessedMode

During the Olympics, it seems like I always come across at least one sport I've never seen or even thought of before—curling, synchronized swimming, race walking, skeleton (that just doesn't sound safe), and more. Even though I'll never compete in these sports, when I watch people who have trained and are accomplishing feats I can hardly imagine, it reminds me how much is possible when we commit to learning, practicing, and persevering—even through failure.

In my daily life, when I work to see the big picture and to broaden my outlook by learning from every experience and persevering, new doors and opportunities open up to me. Those new doors might not lead to me becoming a gold medal synchronized diver, but they might cause me to be a better listener, a better friend, someone with discernment who can help others, or trusted counsel when someone is going through hard times.

When you have success in your life, enjoy it. But also study how you got to that success. Take note of how you prayed, what books you read, what guidance you received, what obstacles you worked through. Those are all important parts of how you continue to grow. And when negative things happen, keep learning! Ask yourself, "How exactly did that go sideways? How can I avoid that in the future?" God is good. He honors a humble heart and will show you His ways.

Don't be afraid to learn and try new things! And don't

be discouraged if you don't get it right the first time. Remain teachable and take godly chances. There is so much out there that God would love to see you doing! And He is with you every moment. After every victory and every defeat, acknowledge Him and *learn*. You got this!

#LevelUpYourFaith

My faith gives me the desire to learn more of Your ways, Lord. Teach me Your ways, my divine Teacher. Direct my path, Lord! Help me to perpetually stay in the process of learning and growing. In Jesus' name I pray, amen.

#GoGetThemBlessings

Thomas Edison is often quoted as saying, "There's a way to do it better . . . find it." What is an area in your life where you feel like you could benefit from finding a better way forward? Write it down and pray about it for the next week. When you look at this again in a week, note what God has revealed to you.

66

Be strong and of a good courage, fear not, nor be afraid of them: for the Lord thy God, he it is that doth go with thee; he will not fail thee, nor forsake thee.
DEUTERONOMY 31:6 KJV

GOD DID IT

God has moved mountains in my life! He has made a way out of no way. One of the biggest mountains He has moved was when He was helping me learn how to forgive my enemies. I would read the Bible verse, "Be kind and helpful to one another, tender-hearted [compassionate, understanding], forgiving one another [readily and freely], just as God in Christ also forgave you" (Ephesians 4:32 AMP)

The devil used to trip me up with arguing and strife with others. But I learned to lean on Jesus and not let my emotions drive my actions. Emotions controlled me sometimes, and I'd make wrong decisions because I was hurt—seeking revenge, holding grudges, paying back pain with pain. But these things only added my wrongdoing on top of theirs, creating a cycle of hurt, pain, and anger.

I didn't want to live that way anymore. I wanted to forgive with intention and move on. It has been so freeing! Forgiveness puts others in God's hands and softens my heart. It brings peace of mind that comes only from the Lord. He makes it happen.

So when people ask, "Hey, Kel, how did you get to where you are? How did you overcome the low times and come back better than before?" my answer is always, "God did it!" I couldn't have achieved any of this or received breakthroughs without God. He has helped me through *everything*. He keeps me encouraged, and

He comforts me during stressful times. I know I can rely on Him every time. Great is God's faithfulness!

There will always be some type of battle, big and small, but God will win it for you *every time*. He did it before, and He can do it again. If you're in a battle right now, still trying to get to victory, don't give up. Fully rely on God and know that He will ultimately be victorious. Keep believing, keep praying, keep trusting. The battle is already won. Have faith to see yourself on the other side of this battle. God will bring the victory!

#LevelUpYourFaith

Thank You, Lord, for never leaving me when I felt lost, confused, or overwhelmed. Your faithfulness gives me courage! Thank You, Lord, for continuing to help me in all things. In Jesus' name I pray, amen.

#GoGetThemBlessings

The battle is won! Whatever battle you are facing, say it out loud. Then say, "I give this battle to You, Lord!" Say it as many times as you need to. Thank God for winning the battle for you and showing you a way forward.

67

Do not conform to the pattern of this world, but be transformed by the renewing of your mind. Then you will be able to test and approve what God's will is—his good, pleasing and perfect will.
ROMANS 12:2

BE TRANSFORMED

#BlessedMode

Do you ever think about how much data is out there on all the computers and phones and tablets in the world? We are all carrying around minicomputers in our hands every day. Sometimes I still can't believe the sheer volume of complex information out there on computers and in the cloud today. When I watched the futuristic cartoon *The Jetsons* as a kid, they communicated using a wristwatch. This magical watch could video chat, make quick calls, and do many other functions that at the time seemed fantastical and impossible. Who knew the producers and writers of a cartoon from the 1960s had imagined what would become a reality for us today? They got it right! People everywhere are wearing smartwatches of some kind.

Our minds are a lot like computers actually. They store a ton of data. Sometimes that data can get a virus—a distraction that causes you to lose your focus, a bad habit that jumbles up the data's truth, negative activities and thoughts that produce negative outcomes. Our minds can be like a computer about to crash if we don't run a software cleanup by renewing our minds daily.

So how do we do that? The first step is: "Do not conform to this world." Because you belong to God, you are not of this world. The desires of this world are often counter to God and will only pollute your mind. The second step is: "Be transformed." You've got to give your life to Christ again and again. Humble your heart.

Get into the Word. Commit to prayer. Let the Holy Spirit work inside you. These things are a daily reboot to keep your operating system running at peak performance.

Start each day with Christ. And as you are obedient and consistent, your refreshed mind will be free from worldly things and will be ready to serve God and bless others with His love.

#LevelUpYourFaith

Help renew my mind, Lord. Clear away all anxiety and distractions. I want to be more like You, Lord. Help me to not conform to the world but to be transformed instead. Give me peace today, a happy heart and a positive mind. In Jesus' name I pray, amen.

#GoGetThemBlessings

Sit quietly and clear your mind of all distractions. Focus on God and let Him speak to your heart and mind. Other thoughts will come in to distract you, but let them pass by like a passing car. When you are done, ask yourself, "How do I feel? What did I think about, and what did God reveal to me?"

68

Search me, God, and know my heart, test me
and know my anxious thoughts.
PSALM 139:23

THE MUSEUM OF YOUR MIND

I sometimes like to imagine that my mind is a museum and that my thoughts—both positive and negative—are like pieces of art, carefully placed in elaborate frames and hung throughout. As God walks through the museum of my mind, spending time in each of the halls and galleries, He sees the thoughts I have created.

When He comes across negative images of myself and others, God lovingly lifts those frames off the wall and removes them. Past, present, or future—if the thought is negative, it needs to be taken down and not left to be observed by others or returned to again and again by me.

In their place, God begins to hang more pleasing, positive images—images of the thoughts He has for me—that I am His beloved, that He has great plans for me, that He delights in me. The museum of my mind becomes pleasing, beautiful, and filled with lovely, godly thoughts. As God carefully hangs these positive images, a shift takes place—I begin to be filled with His thoughts and His ways. I feel hopeful. I'm less anxious. I can see the blessings all around me that I might have missed before when my mind museum was cluttered with negativity. I can see the good in others and the ways I can help them and love them. God comes alongside me and says, "Isn't this better?" And it is.

What does the museum of your mind look like? Is it filled with lovely thoughts? Are you focusing on "whatever is true, whatever is noble, whatever is right, whatever is pure, whatever is lovely, whatever is admirable" (Philippians 4:8)? Or is your mind filled with anxiety and worry, negativity, or fear? Remember that God made you—He designed each of us individually, which means He designed *your mind* to do amazing things.

We are capable of so much when we have God in our thoughts and in our lives.

#LevelUpYourFaith

My thoughts are Your thoughts, Lord. Renew my mind each day. Help me to see myself the way You see me. Help me to see others the way You see them as well. Today I will focus on things that are true, holy, peaceful, and praiseworthy. In Jesus' name I pray, amen.

#GoGetThemBlessings

Let God be your spiritual art critic in the museum of your mind. Ask yourself, *What is taking my focus away from God?* Then remove those things that are blurring your focus, and do the things that help you keep your focus on Christ. Leave your Bible open around the house. Read devotionals and uplifting books. Listen to a positive podcast. Play worship music. When you ask God to direct your thoughts, He will give you opportunities to find Him everywhere.

69

Christ gives me the strength to face anything.
PHILIPPIANS 4:13 CEV

UNSTOPPABLE

Hey, you. Yeah, I'm talking to you.

Who told you to stop going? Who said you could quit? What made you think it was time to tap out?

Don't stop! Keep going! *Refuse* to stop. Go after that dream in your heart. Say out loud, "I serve an unstoppable God. My God is unstoppable, which makes me unstoppable." Climb that mountain and yell out, "I refuse to stop!"

Only you know what your mountain is. Only you know what you need to conquer and what obstacles might lie in your path. And whatever that mountain is? The Lord says it is yours. Even mountains quake in His presence! (Nahum 1:5). Surely He can help with whatever you're trying to conquer. You just have to believe and keep going.

So why are you stopping? This is a reminder to not stop. Go be who God told you to be.

Philippians 4:13 is such a powerful verse. I want you to remember the promise for you in this verse—you can do *all* things through Christ who strengthens you. All things! Not just some things. You can do all things with God. For that to happen, you need to spend a lot of time learning from Jesus, so spend time with Him, studying His Word, praying, just being together. Don't get distracted from His presence by focusing on things that will slow down or completely stop your spiritual drive. Don't let anyone or anything extinguish the fire God placed in your spirit to chase the vision He has for you.

So go get them blessings! Switch to Blessed Mode! Let's go!

#LevelUpYourFaith

I will go after those things You tell me to, Lord. Make them clear to me. Light my path. Show me how to be unstoppable with You. I will never stop giving You all the glory. In Jesus' name I pray, amen.

#GoGetThemBlessings

Create a vision board of images, pictures, and affirmations of the dreams and desires God has given you. Let this serve as motivation and to keep you focused on where God wants you to go. At the top of the board, write "Blessed Mode!"

we don't yet see things clearly. We're squinting in a fog, peering through a mist. But it won't be long before the weather clears and the sun shines bright! We'll see it all then, see it all as clearly as God sees us, knowing him directly just as he knows us!
1 CORINTHIANS 13:12 MSG

RITUAL VISION

#BlessedMode

When I was a kid, I couldn't see the chalkboard clearly in class. It turned out that I needed to see an eye doctor. And what we discovered when I finally saw one is that I had been walking around with my own understanding of how life looked, but I wasn't really seeing it clearly. The way I could see was the only thing I knew. I didn't even realize how bad it was! And when it came time to solve this issue so I could finally see things the right way, I had to go to someone who could help me with my vision problem—an eye doctor.

I was able to get help with my eyesight. I did not stay in that problem. But sometimes in life, when a problem comes up, we make the mistake of not seeking out help. Perhaps we think this is just the way things are. Or maybe we know it's a problem, but we think we can fix it ourselves. Instead of getting correct instruction or help, we ignore the people who could help, who could give us helpful advice. Even worse, sometimes we ignore the Holy Spirit inside of us, telling us to seek the kingdom of God first. Don't make that mistake!

If I had continued to let my vision go without seeking help, I would have hindered myself from learning and missed out on new levels of knowledge and understanding. I would have bumped into walls. I would have struggled in sports. I wouldn't have received a driver's license when I got older. I would have missed out on so much!

Our spiritual vision needs to be addressed. Just think about what you could be missing out on because your spiritual vision is blurry. So let's solve the vision problem in our lives! Don't waste any more time stumbling around in the darkness with no vision or purpose. Ask for help from our Lord to grow in knowledge and understanding and see Him and the big picture clearly. Let's go for that 20/20 vision with God!

#LevelUpYourFaith

I see with new eyes, Lord! I see the bigger picture. Continue to help me see what You see. In Jesus' name I pray, amen.

#GoGetThemBlessings

Grab a pair of sunglasses and go outside or into your backyard. If you are reading this at night, wait until the sun is out in the morning. Go outside and just look up at the sky, admiring all that God has created while taking your sunglasses on and off (but don't look directly into the sun!). Focus on the scripture in the message today, 1 Corinthians 13:12.

71

But grow in the grace and knowledge of our Lord and Savior Jesus Christ. To him be glory both now and forever! Amen.
2 PETER 3:18

STAY OUT OF YOUR LANE

#BlessedMode

I'm not a fan of the saying "Stay in your lane," which means to stick with what you know and what you are good at. Now don't get me wrong. There is some truth to the statement. When people speak about things they don't know and pretend like they do, that can lead to folly, mistakes, and big accidents in life.

I want to talk about people who abuse "stay in your lane" as a way to hold others back and put them in a box. Don't let people put you in a box. With God, your opportunities are limitless! Stay willing to learn new and try new things, even if there are naysayers. Expand your mind! God has so much to teach you, and this beautiful world is full of knowledge and mysteries just waiting to be learned. Do not be afraid to get out there and do something different. You have the ability to make a huge difference doing something that's a stretch for you. So get after those blessings!

Because God made each of us unique, things that may be difficult for some people to learn won't be difficult for you. As your spiritual maturity grows, God will continue to give you wisdom and divine discernment. What is crooked for others will be made straight for you. And where you may have struggled in the past, you will find new breakthroughs. This has happened so much in my own life!

People may say "stay in your lane" because they're scared you might take their place. They see you moving and prospering, and they start to worry that you'll be in competition. In God's holy world though, there is a position for all of us. So keep chasing those dreams.

The writer of Proverbs said, "For wisdom will come into your heart, and knowledge will be pleasant to your soul" (2:10 ESV). Knowledge is something that no one can take from you, so learn all that you can. And once you've learned in one lane, switch to another and learn something new, and then to another. As you keep learning and growing and switching lanes, God will take you to new levels as you grow and serve Him more.

#LevelUpYourFaith

God, You designed my mind to learn many different things. I ask that You would make the brain You have given me healthy. Keep it free from any anxiety or setbacks. I pray for a clear and pure mind to be ready to move in positive directions and create the things You want me to create. In Jesus' name I pray, amen.

#GoGetThemBlessings

Is there something you've been wanting to learn? Go ahead—try something new. Learn a new song. A new word. A new language. How to play an instrument. Find something positive and new to do today.

But truly God has listened; he has attended to the voice of my prayer.

PSALM 66:19 ESV

72

SEEK WISDOM

#BlessedMode

How can making hurried, emotionally driven decisions delay you from reaching your goal? Think about this example: You have a to-do list that you have been following, but someone asks you to do something else or take on a new opportunity. You're stressed because you keep asking yourself if this is a good move or a bad move. This new thing doesn't match up with your goals, with your to-do list.

At a time like this, I encourage you not to be pressured to give a quick answer. Now, I'm not talking about emergencies that might come up and need to be handled immediately. That's a separate matter. I'm talking about opportunities that *sound* good but might not actually be good for you.

So how do you know if a new opportunity you didn't plan for is right for you? First, stop and think before you make the decision. It's okay to stop, think, and pray about it. God always knows the answer, so always go to Him first. And let yourself have time to hear from Him. He will help you weigh the pros and cons and will make the answer clear for you.

Second, don't worry about the person or business that wants to work with you or team up with you. If it's someone you should be connecting with, they'll respect you taking time to think and pray about it. (One bit of advice: don't say you'll take time to pray if you know the answer is no right away. Sometimes it's tempting to say, "Let me go pray about it," just to get people off our backs. That's not helpful to anyone.)

A big decision on the horizon? Honestly pray and seek God's will, and He'll guide your steps. And whatever the answer is—yes or no—it will be the right move because you heard from God.

#LevelUpYourFaith

Heavenly Father, You know me and You know every opportunity that is brought to me. I bring these things to You to see if I should pursue them. You know what is right and what is good for me. I will continue to make my requests known to You so I can focus on the next move I need to make. You are my perfect Guide. In Jesus' name I pray, amen.

#GoGetThemBlessings

Take time right now to get clarity on something you've been wondering about—a big move, a new job, a new health plan. Whatever it is, tell God your concerns and wait for an answer. God says, "Call to me and I will answer you, and will tell you great and hidden things that you have not known" (Jeremiah 33:3 ESV).

Then they cried unto the Lord in their trouble, and he delivered them out of their distresses.

PSALM 107:6 KJV

73

HE DELIVERS

#BlessedMode

God delivers us from extreme anxiety, sorrow, and pain— otherwise known as distress. Notice how today's verse says plural "distresses," not singular "distress." I don't know a single person who has ever had only one distress in life! You will have to defeat and confront and address many different challenges in life. After you're done with one obstacle, just give it a little time, and you'll be asking God to help you with another.

There's so much good news here though! God *never* says, "I helped you already! You got too much going on, and I do not have time to pray with you *every single day* to get you out of distress after distress." No! God is *always* ready to help! He loves it when you come to Him—no matter how often or how much help you need. The real question is whether you're ready to go to Him to get the help.

Today's verse also says, "They cried unto the Lord in their trouble." Pay attention to this part: *in their trouble*. You could have anxiety, sorrow, or pain going on, and as it's happening—in that very moment—God is with you. He is there. You can reach out to Him while you are in it.

So don't get discouraged or stop calling out His name. These words can be a refrain on your lips at all times: "Lord, I need You! Deliver me from this!"

Then once you are delivered, thank Him, move forward in His grace and purpose, and put that struggle behind you. You might say, "Pastor Kel, this is so hard to do." In your own power? Yeah, it is hard. But remember this: *nothing* is too hard for God (Jeremiah 32:17). And you aren't doing this alone. He is by your side and He delivers us every time.

Nothing is too hard for You, God! Everything is possible. I have hope and I have faith. I keep moving forward, pushing toward the goal You have for me. Your Word is manifesting in my life. I give You the glory!

Let God be your motivation to keep pushing through distress. Nothing is impossible and nothing is too hard for God. When you begin to feel doubtful, say to yourself, "Nothing is too hard for God."

74

SPIRITUAL SELF-CARE

The weapons we fight with are not the weapons of the world. On the contrary, they have divine power to demolish strongholds. We demolish arguments and every pretension that sets itself up against the knowledge of God, and we take captive every thought to make it obedient to Christ.
2 CORINTHIANS 10:4–5

#BlessedMode

I did an interview in 2020 in which the reporter asked me how I felt about all the anger, confusion, and unforgiveness going on that year. Here was my answer:

> People need to remember that they are spiritual beings who also require spiritual care, especially during the pandemic. This is spiritual warfare that's going on. We have to realize that we're all spirits. We have to look through the whole skin and anything—titles and all that stuff—and just really pull everything back and be transparent about it and understand that we're all spiritual. And the thing about it is that we need to respond in love like our Lord and Savior. If we focus on that, that's when real change will happen. That's when real empathy will happen; that's when you start to look at others in a different way. You start to look at your choices in a different way, and that different way is in a positive way, a blissful way, a calming way, a soothing way for others. I feel that with the world today, anger needs to be gone. And the only reason there is a lot of anger and a lot of anxiety is because there is fearfulness of the unknown. But when you know that the victory is won through Christ . . . He's going to get you through those troubles.

Let the church say amen!

#LevelUpYourFaith

Father, I recognize that there is spiritual warfare going on and that I need Your skills to teach me how to battle. With You, I will win every time! I won't try to fight the battle on my own. I will fight by letting You lead and by trusting and believing in Your wonderful power. I know You will get me to the victory each time!

#GoGetThemBlessings

Anger hurts you more than the person who upset you. Search your heart today and see if you find any unforgiveness. If you do, quickly forgive that person. Just say their name out loud: "I forgive _____ in the name of Jesus," and visualize the anger dripping off of you. I have done this, and so much weight was lifted off my shoulders.

75

Do all things without complaining and disputing.
PHILIPPIANS 2:14 NKJV

NO COMPLAINTS

#BlessedMode

It really stinks to see somebody pray for something like a job, and when they get the job, they get comfortable and start to complain. They say things like, "I'm getting up too early," "This job is boring," and, "I don't have time to do what I want to do," and "This job is too much."

Not that long ago they were anxiously praying to get that job they're complaining about! They're making money. They got what they prayed for. And yet . . . they continue to give off negative energy. Rather than being thankful that God blessed them with the job they wanted, they complain and bring negativity to the people in their lives and to the workplace too. Have you ever known someone like that? A good thing is never good enough.

On the other end of the spectrum, there's that person who appreciates his job, brings positivity, and brightens up the room. It's like the character Kel Kimble, who I played on Nickelodeon's *Kenan & Kel*. Kel never complained when Kenan Rockmore would ask him to do all these crazy tasks at the end of the show. Kel never responded with a complaint. He just said, "Aww, here it goes," and he would do the task that was presented to him.

I know that was a TV show, but I think it's something we should pay attention to. So try it! Be that person. Brighten up the room. Don't complain. Find the joy in everything you do and see what happens in your heart and in the lives around you.

Thank You for waking me up this morning, Lord. I am thankful for all You have done for me and are doing for me. Today I will find joy in everything I do. I will not complain. In Jesus' name I pray, amen.

#GoGetThemBlessings

Look at yourself in the mirror and say out loud, "Today is the day that the Lord has made. I will rejoice and be glad in it" (Psalm 118:24). Continue to say it no matter what happened last night or even a few minutes ago. Just keep saying it until you feel joy. Smile while you are doing it. Find the joy!

76

HEALING WILL COME

For God, who said, "Let light shine out of darkness," has shone in our hearts to give the light of the knowledge of the glory of God in the face of Jesus Christ.
2 CORINTHIANS 4:6 ESV

#BlessedMode

Light reveals whatever is hiding in the dark. But how you absorb what is revealed to you, how you react to what you find . . . *that* is one of the hardest parts of seeing the world with new eyes. I think that's the "spiritual maturity" believers talk about (which is not always fun!).

As you grow in faith and are challenged by God, you'll be hit by issues and frustrations. You'll be faced with darkness. But you are a new person in God! Perspective, knowledge, wisdom, and faith have to be part of your next move instead of leaning solely on your emotions. For me, that has meant learning to take a breath, keep my mouth shut (that part is hard!), and listen for what God desires for me in that circumstance. When someone disappoints me, I still sometimes want to pop off and respond immediately, but I've gotten better at learning to stay silent and call on God for wisdom. Knowledge and healing start there.

When you first get rocked with crazy news or find out something shocking, you can feel hurt or betrayed. For me, it's like everything goes to black and white, and the color is stripped away. I don't talk about everything that has happened to me, but I've had a lot of traumatic experiences in life. Anger and discouragement were my go-to emotions, which made everything look negative. I can promise you that as you continue to mature in Christ, the moments after a devastation come with "healing in

166

the revealing"—a process that might take some time but will have unbelievable results if you stick with Christ. God has helped me heal from more than I can even believe, and He will do it for you too.

You can get through hardships with God's help. You can find light in the darkness. Sometimes it seems unlikely or even impossible. But I know this is true because God's Word is true. Your future will shine bright as you heal and grow from your experiences, as you gain wisdom and understanding, and as God shines the light of His love on your life.

#LevelUpYourFaith

Thank You for healing me, Lord. Thank You for helping me grow spiritually and helping me see the brighter side of it all. Please continue to comfort me on this journey. In Jesus' name I pray, amen.

#GoGetThemBlessings

The next time you get some shocking news or become upset, give yourself a "rant window"—some time to talk to God and vent before talking to the person who caused the trouble. God can handle your frustration and anger. And this will give you time and guidance so you can have a mature and positive response when you're finally ready to talk about it. Talk to God first.

77

The LORD is my rock and my fortress and my deliverer.
2 SAMUEL 22:2 ESV

SPECIAL DELIVERY

#BlessedMode

My wife, Asia, and I love online shopping. After 2020, I'm guessing we all love it a little more than any of us expected (and are super grateful for all the people who make it possible). Although you might not get the item as immediately as if you walked in the store, online shopping is so fast now that sometimes things show up in only a day or two. I've even had something show up *the same day* I ordered it—how are they even doing that? I sometimes wonder if my online shopping cart can hear me thinking about those sweet new kicks and just orders them for me, LOL.

I'm not totally sure how all the shipping companies handle these priority deliveries, but back in the olden days (of just a few years ago!), an item that arrived faster than regular first-class mail was referred to as a "special delivery." The definition of *deliver* is "something promised or expected." So what if we apply that to our prayer requests and the many blessings God gives us?

When you pray, you can know a few things without a doubt: God is listening, He cares, and He will answer. Now, we don't always know what those answers will be or how they will look, but we know He will deliver—and it will always be on time. Same-day delivery is no sweat for God. He meets us with what He has promised *in the moment we ask.*

So call on Him. Trust Him to deliver. And don't be surprised when He sends you blessings you didn't even see coming.

#LevelUpYourFaith

Lord, You always deliver on Your promises, and You deliver blessings into my hands and in my life. I will not doubt. You always make a way where there is no way. You know me, and You know my heart. I have faith in Your words. In Jesus' name I pray, amen.

#GoGetThemBlessings

Whatever date and time you are reading this, go grab a piece of paper and jot down some dreams you are praying for. Put the paper in an envelope and say a prayer over it. Seal the envelope and write "special delivery" on the front. Tuck this envelope away, and don't open it for a year. I can't wait to know what special deliveries God will bring your way when you open it a year from now.

78

BE TEACHABLE

#BlessedMode

Sometimes learning doesn't sound fun. It means buckling down, listening to someone else, being open to new ideas, and sometimes even struggling through the new material. But when you belong to God, the learning never ends so we may as well learn to love being teachable.

I actually feel like the school of God's ways is the most rewarding work I've ever done. I can't think of a time when I've needed to know the square root of something in my daily life, but every lesson I have learned at God's feet has served me—whether that lesson was purely beautiful or whether it came through hardship or mistakes.

When you've made mistakes and need help, look to God. Today's verse reminds us that we become wiser when we take instruction. In the times when I've really messed up, I needed God's instruction! God is still with you regardless of whatever mess you may have gotten yourself into, and He will help you learn from it. He doesn't go anywhere, especially when you've made mistakes. Look at mistakes as the teachable moments they are, and God will honor your humble and willing heart. And once you've learned, once you know better, you can do better the next time. You have insight and experience, and more than that, you have godly wisdom.

So don't let the mistakes break you down; let them teach you! Remember, there are no failures, only lessons. When a mistake happens, talk to the Lord. "Lord, what are You teaching me at this moment?" Don't dwell on the mistake or begin cataloging all the ways you've messed up in the past. Instead, say, "Okay, what did I learn from this? And how can I be better now? Lord, show me what You want me to do."

Heeding this wisdom and practicing it in my own life has made me the man that I am today. I won't say it was easy. I had to do the work of having a humble and open heart. But I know you can do this. And as you learn and work through setbacks, you will have an amazing, beautiful, and divine comeback—with God right there, cheering you on.

#LevelUpYourFaith

You remind me, Lord, that I am not a failure. I am encouraged and motivated by Your love for me, and every day I have a chance to do better than the day before. Thank You for every teachable moment. With You I am unstoppable! In Jesus' name I pray, amen.

#GoGetThemBlessings

Think about some of the mistakes you've learned from and the techniques you now use to not make those mistakes again. Give yourself a hug for surviving your mistakes, for learning from them, and for now letting them go.

79

SEE WHAT CAN BE

Where there is no vision, the people perish: but he that keepeth the law, happy is he.
PROVERBS 29:18 KJV

#BlessedMode

I was putting in my contacts the other morning and thinking about why I wear them and how long it's been. I've been putting contacts on my eyes since my early teens, which is a decent amount of time (I'll let you do that math!). I'm near-sighted, which means I can't see far away. I can see close objects clearly (like a book), while distant objects appear blurry. Without my contacts, I'm stumbling around a room, trying to make my way through a bunch of fuzzy objects. If you have to wear glasses or contacts, you know what this is like and how disorienting it can be.

When I think about this in a spiritual sense, it's a lot like how I need the spiritual lenses the Holy Spirit provides to reveal what I can't see with my own eyes. I need to take on God's sight so I can see all the possibilities He sees, and I need to get understanding and insight through His eyes. When I do this, I can see my abilities and potential clearly. I can see His purpose for me. I can see where He can use me.

Are there areas in your life where you feel like God has clearly shown you His will for your life? What has that experience been like? Are there areas where the world around you—and the next steps you're supposed to take—are fuzzy and have you staggering through a blurry fog, looking for clarity? Don't forget that God is by your side for just these moments.

And what could actually be if you could see with God's lenses, with the help of God's perfect vision? Let's find out!

Help me see what You see, Lord. I want to see people the way You see them, as Your creation, beloved by You. Help me to make choices based on proper insight and discernment from You, Lord. In Jesus' name I pray, amen.

#GoGetThemBlessings

It's believed that the philosopher Seneca said, "Every new beginning comes from some other beginning's end." Even if something is over, that just means another beginning has started. So stop focusing on the past and instead focus your vision on what is possible with God. A great new beginning is right in front of you.

80

Commit your work to the Lord, and your plans will be established.
PROVERBS 16:3 ESV

JUGGLE THAT FOCUS

I have spent many years training myself to juggle the demands of life positively and not to get distracted by negative thoughts. Not long ago, my training was put to the test when I got a call from my agent with a big audition.

"It's tomorrow afternoon, and you need to be off-book."

Okay.

Off-book means all written lines for my character needed to be memorized before the audition. I usually like to have two days to prepare for off-book auditions, and it was already evening, which meant I needed to add learning my lines to the list of other tasks for the next morning—my sermon, bullet points for a meeting, the demands of being a father and a husband, and more.

I wanted to give it a try, though, so I created a to-do list before bed and got up early the next morning. I arrived at my audition ready to go. It went well. I even got a few compliments from the casting directors. But two days passed, and I was still thinking about that audition. *Why haven't I heard anything?*

I found out later that I didn't get the role. I was really disappointed, but the Lord gave me peace, pushing me to focus on what I'd learned instead of on what I'd lost. The preparation had revealed that my discipline and memory skills have improved, and I juggled that crazy day without dropping one task. I just needed to drop the negative thoughts.

Have you ever experienced anything like this? Maybe you worked really hard for something and it didn't end like you'd hoped. Maybe a friendship fell apart and you can't stop thinking about it. Or something happened at work that you can't stop replaying in your head. In those moments, we have the opportunity to thank God for helping us learn, for placing dreams in our hearts and giving us a bigger purpose for Him, even if the road there isn't what we expected.

#LevelUpYourFaith

Lord, help me let go of negative thoughts and patterns that take my focus away from You. You are my divine day planner. I will consult You first in everything I do because You know my future. Today I will keep only what You want me to keep and receive only what You want me to receive. In Jesus' name I pray, amen.

#GoGetThemBlessings

Now, let's actually release the negative thoughts that are distracting you. Name the thought and take authority over it: Father, take _____ from my thoughts. I will not dwell on _____ anymore. I am free from _____. My thoughts, spirit, soul, and body belong to You, Lord. I am made righteous by the blood of Your Son, Jesus. Write this down and put it somewhere where you'll see it often.

81

COACHED BY THE WAY MAKER

For our struggle is not against flesh and blood, but against the rulers, against the authorities, against the powers of this dark world and against the spiritual forces of evil in the heavenly realms.
EPHESIANS 6:12

#BlessedMode

Have you ever played on a team of any kind? Or perhaps you've been coached outside of a sports setting, maybe by a mentor or teacher who guided you in academic or professional pursuits. Coaches unite their teams; they provide strategy and foresight; they challenge the team members to work hard, to be inspired, to reach for the impossible. Some of my favorite movies over the years have included a coach who just didn't give up on his or her team.

You may not have a flesh-and-bones coach in your life at this moment, but guess what you do have? The ultimate Coach: the Lord.

- He sees your weakness and can reveal the ways in which you can grow stronger.
- His strategy is to prosper you, to give you hope and a future.
- He fights for you always, even if you have not yet called on Him.
- He makes a way when you can't see one and lights the path before you.

So when you head to your corner of the ring, fatigued from battle of everyday life, use that time of rest to be rejuvenated by God's Word, to pray for wisdom, and to seek encouragement.

And when that break is over, jump right back in with your Coach cheering you on, knowing that you can "trust in the win"—that the Lord will wipe away the hurt, the pain, and the pressure from whatever situations you're enduring. Yes, you may have to fight. No, it won't always be easy. But your Coach is there, making a way where there was none.

Don't forget: our fight is against much more than earthly troubles. We are fighting in the spiritual realm, with the power of God alongside us.

#LevelUpYourFaith

You are the Way Maker, God! My faith and Your presence in my life will be made known to everyone who sees the victorious breakthroughs You bring about in my life. Thank You for being my Coach and for never leaving my side. In Jesus' name I pray, amen.

#GoGetThemBlessings

Faith must be active, or it will wither away—so let's take action! Meditate on this verse: "You see that his faith and his actions were working together, and his faith was made complete by what he did" (James 2:22). Are your faith and actions working together? If not, jot down some areas where your actions could align more closely with your faith. Tackle some of these this week.

82

THE GOOD FIGHT

repay no one evil for evil, but give thought to do what is honorable in the sight of all. If possible, so far as it depends on you, live peaceably with all. Beloved, never avenge yourselves, but leave it to the wrath of God, for it is written, "Vengeance is mine, I will repay, says the Lord." To the contrary, "if your enemy is hungry, feed him; if he is thirsty, give him something to drink; for by so doing you will heap burning coals on his head." Do not be overcome by evil, but overcome evil with good.
ROMANS 12:17–21 ESV

#BlessedMode

Today's Bible verse says to overcome evil with good. Easier said than done sometimes, I know. But when we overcome evil with good, when we pray for the evil that the Enemy tried to use against us to be gone, we fight the good fight of faith.

Another way we can fight for good is to pray for our enemies to not be destroyed, but instead to repent and give their lives to Christ. That's a double hit to Satan! He loses the battle of our mind *and* our spirit when we use the weapon within us, the Holy Spirit, to counter his attack. We do not try to handle it ourselves and return evil with evil. That will just lead to more heartache, loss, and confusion. No, we do what is good, we stay peaceful, and we use our faith, letting the Lord handle it.

And trust me, the Lord goes full heavyweight boxer on negative spirits, destructive strongholds, and dark shadows that try to entangle us in the spiritual realm. He breaks down that evil, knocking it all the way off of us! He fights our battles and takes care of His children.

If you're facing a challenge, or feeling like the Enemy is attacking you, instead of fighting evil with evil, try fighting evil with something good and pure. Fight the good fight.

178

Lord, thank You for working on my behalf. Thank You for protecting me. Thank You for not allowing the Enemy to drag me to hell! I will follow and listen to You always. In Jesus' name I pray, amen.

#GoGetThemBlessings

Do some shadow boxing. Basically, punch the air until you get tired. You can even imagine boxing with a problem you're facing. Then, think of 1 Corinthians 9:26, which says, "I do not fight like a boxer beating the air." You can't win against the air or against an enemy you can't see. But the Lord sees all things and fights for you.

83

You belong to God and have already won your fight with those who are against Christ because there is someone in your hearts who is stronger than any evil teacher in this wicked world.
1 JOHN 4:4 TLB

PREPARE TO LEVEL UP

#BlessedMode

Sometimes life brings pain. As much as we might not like it, pain is inevitable. But the pain is preparation! As you walk through those valleys, you're being prepped for the next phase of life. Whatever lesson you learn, whatever resilience you build, whatever new closeness you develop with the Lord—it helps you "level up" the next time you encounter a challenge.

We all want to level up. But first you gotta beat the level! You can't skip a level (and if you do, it'll come back to you later . . . trust me). You have to learn everything about the level of life you're in right now, and trust that God is lighting your pathway. He will show you how to navigate that level so you can move on to the next with growth. But beware: when you do it without Him, you'll get off balance and stumble and get stuck on a level while everyone else is moving up and up.

It's like when Jesus walked on water in Matthew 14:22–33. Peter wanted to do it too. "Come on out here," Jesus said. Peter stepped right out, but then he took his eyes off Jesus and got scared by the wind and began to sink. What I like about that story is that Jesus said "Come on out here" because he knew Peter was designed to walk on water just like Him. But *it was up to Peter to believe* in what Jesus could do through him.

God is gonna take you places. Trust me. He'll take you places you never imagined possible! But you have to believe, focus, and keep your eyes on Him so you don't lose your balance. And don't forget that greater is He who is in you than he who is in the world (see John 4:4).

#LevelUpYourFaith

I will keep watch and manage my life by following Your agenda, Lord! Strategic prayer and divine awareness are important to me. I want to download success from You into my life and detach myself from evil. In Jesus' name I pray, amen.

#GoGetThemBlessings

Grab some index cards and write the name of each book of the Bible on a card. Include how many chapters each book has. For example, "Proverbs, 32 chapters." Turn the cards upside down and shuffle them a few times to get them all mixed up. Then randomly pick two cards and do push-ups for one and jumping jacks for the other. If you selected Proverbs with 32 chapters and the book of Psalms with 150 chapters, decide whether to do 32 push-ups and 150 jumping jacks or 150 push-ups and 32 jumping jacks. It's a great way to focus on God, and at the end of the workout, you can read a verse from each book you picked.

84

HEALTHY HABITS

watch and pray so that you will not fall into temptation.
The spirit is willing, but the flesh is weak."
MATTHEW 26:41

The devil knows the buttons to push and the emotions to hit with us, and he knows our habitual sins—the ones that linger for years, sometimes a lifetime, if they're not taken care of. It is those sinful habits that come up when we're squeezed with the pressures of life, causing us to backslide right into things we thought we would not do again. Maybe it's lies, anger, substance abuse, harm to ourselves or others, or lustful thoughts or actions. There are so many that can trap us.

When we find ourselves back doing something we thought we overcame, it is disheartening, and we feel guilty. And the devil loves that. He wants to keep us in our sin, feeling guilty and thinking we can never overcome it. But I am here to tell you, if you are truly trying to erase the habitual sin that sneaks up when you are stressed out or under pressure, God will help you. Quickly ask for forgiveness, and then ask for help. God will give you a divine idea. I know this because He has done it for me. He taught me to change my reactions, to change the patterns I used to follow when I was overwhelmed. He reminded me to always be on guard because that sin will try its best to get my attention again and again.

A *habit* is anything you do repeatedly. So to get better at changing our reactions and patterns, we have to practice a new habit multiple times to make it stick. Every habit is based on a loop with a trigger that starts it. Learn what the trigger is so that whenever you feel the urge to jump back into the habit, you have a cue to wake up spiritually. Get up, walk around, and pray at that moment so you can break the habit and replace it with a godlier, positive habit.

Recognize your habitual sin, call it by name, give it to Jesus, and ask Him to help you let go of it. Ask Him to keep it away from you by making your thoughts His thoughts, which are so much more pure, kind, and loving than ours. And when you feel the pressure to fall back into your old ways, remember what you practiced and discussed with God.

#LevelUpYourFaith

We are creatures of habit, Lord, and sometimes that includes bad habits. Help me remember to come to You, Lord, as I seek to replace bad habits with good ones. Keep me alert and out of zombie mode. Put my spirit in control of my flesh! In Jesus' name I pray, amen.

#GoGetThemBlessings

Some habitual sin happens because of our surroundings, so if that is a problem for you, change your environment. What might be influencing the bad habit? *Change it.* Jot down how that habit makes you feel. It took a long time to develop that bad habit, and it won't be undone overnight. Remember that God will give you strength.

85

NO HIDING

Such people are false apostles, deceitful workers, masquerading as apostles of Christ. And no wonder, for Satan himself masquerades as an angel of light. It is not surprising, then, if his servants also masquerade as servants of righteousness. Their end will be what their actions deserve.
2 CORINTHIANS 11:13–15

#BlessedMode

How do we know if someone is living by the Spirit of God? We're outside looking in at them, and we don't know their deepest desires, but God does. He knows the true desires of their heart. The verses in 2 Corinthians tell us that there is some fakery going on under this flesh. People are allowing themselves to be controlled by the Enemy and are hiding behind a persona or mask. That is why Paul tells us as believers to put on the Lord Jesus Christ and make no provision for the flesh, to gratify its desires (Romans 13:14). The Psalmist says to delight yourself in the Lord—not the flesh—and He will give you the desires of your heart (Psalm 37:4).

I remember when 2019 was ending and everyone was saying, "The year 2020 will be the year of vision, and everything will be revealed! We'll see clearly in 2020." But no one knew it would be our spiritual selves being revealed! The literal masks that we put on during the pandemic covered up the metaphorical masks that the Enemy used to trick us. We had masks over masks! So what were we left with? People couldn't use the same persona as before to hide their true selves and their hidden sin. And since we were forced to stay home, that made us spend more time with who we really are. What did we find out about ourselves in the quiet time, while being quarantined? What was revealed to you?

It was a time to sit and *be* your true self, and for some that was torture. For some, they missed wearing their spiritual mask too much. For others, it was overwhelming to face the stress from the spiritual warfare that was going on inside them. It seemed like everyone had a full-on therapy session with their spirit and their flesh during this pandemic. And God said, "I have you, so repent, move away from sin, and forgive yourself." Stop hiding behind the mask! Face yourself—with your face uncovered—and face God too. Ask for His help, and He will reveal Himself to you.

#LevelUpYourFaith

Lord, I will tell the truth and face my true self, because nothing is covered up that will not be revealed or hidden that will not be known. You make all things known. In Jesus' name I pray, amen.

#GoGetThemBlessings

Use a dry-erase marker to write positive, kind words about yourself on your bathroom mirror, words that you think Jesus would say to you (He loves you so much!). Look at yourself and see those words across your face as an artful reminder that you are loved and made in His image.

86 — NO LIE

God is not a man, so he does not lie. He is not human, so he does not change his mind. Has he ever spoken and failed to act? Has he ever promised and not carried it through?
NUMBERS 23:19 NLT

#BlessedMode

The Lord cannot and does not lie. When He says He will help you, He will. If you ask, it will be given to you. It will happen.

I had an audition for a cop show that would shoot in New Orleans, and I didn't get the job. I was devastated, but I had to stay patient and trust that God would give me another opportunity. During the audition, it was almost like God shut my mouth. I couldn't remember my lines at all! I was frustrated, but I didn't get mad at God.

Psalm 5:3 says, "Listen to my voice in the morning, LORD. Each morning I bring my requests to you and wait expectantly" (NLT). I knew I needed to be patient. The Lord knew my requests. I spoke them every morning: Bills paid. Good paying job. Stay happy.

A while later, I was asked to honor a producer I had worked with at an award show. Now, me and this person didn't always see eye to eye, but I had forgiven him and went to the award show and presented him with the award. It just so happened that he was casting a new show . . . and he wanted me to audition for it. Would you believe that I got that show? And other jobs and opportunities started to happen from booking that job! The things that started unfolding only could have happened with me in Los Angeles, not if I had booked the cop show in New Orleans. And if I hadn't forgiven that producer, if I had burned a bridge with him, the chances of us building something new together would have been real slim. But I purposed to remain righteous and obedient in God's sight, and God rewarded my patience, sacrifice, and endurance.

In the moments of disappointment, frustration, and even fear, I had to have faith that God was working for me, even when it seemed like nothing was working out. I had to know that God was true to His word, that He fulfills His promises. I know you've been in those situations too. Trust God, and trust that you will receive endless blessings. You will see them happen right before your eyes, my friend!

#LevelUpYourFaith

Thank You so much, Lord, for not changing Your mind. Thank You for not failing to act. All Your promises are true! I am so happy that You love me and that You saved me. In Jesus' name I pray, amen.

#GoGetThemBlessings

Recall a lie that was told to you and how it made you feel. Then reflect on some of the truths God has told you. Now thank Him for never lying to you.

SIPPING TEA

> Everyone who drinks of this water will be thirsty again, but whoever drinks of the water that I will give him will never be thirsty again. The water that I will give him will become in him a spring of water welling up to eternal life."
>
> **JOHN 4:13–14** ESV

#BlessedMode

I love to unwind and sip on some tea. It's so relaxing to me. I love all different types, especially the teas that cause my body and mind to calm down and de-stress.

You've probably seen that meme of Kermit the Frog sipping tea (it's a whole other kind of tea sipping, LOL). The look on his face is disbelief, and at the bottom of the meme it says, "But that's none of my business." That meme is so funny to me and so true. It's like, "I see you over there doing people wrong, but I'm not tryna include myself in your foolishness and make it of my business. I'm going to continue to relax and sip my tea."

As believers, we need to take that idea to heart. It's really easy to let ourselves get swept up in gossip, negative behaviors, and other things that can really hurt others and ourselves (and our witness for God!). There are some things we just don't need to mix up in. We need to keep our God-given peace and let no one disrupt it.

The other thing that cracks me up about the sipping-Kermit meme is that frogs don't even drink through their mouths. He can't even sip that Lipton, guys! That's right—frogs don't drink like we do; they absorb water directly through their skin in an area known as a "drinking patch" located on their bellies and the underside of their thighs. Isn't that cool? And isn't God's creation amazing?

I think we can learn even more from that revelation. Like a frog, I want to absorb God's goodness and be filled with His courage, wisdom, love, and presence throughout my entire being. I want the Holy Spirit to surround me and fill me so that I don't thirst. Let's be more like frogs and soak in God's provision as we swim through life.

#LevelUpYourFaith

Fill me with Your love, Holy Spirit, and pour Your greatness and loving understanding into my heart! I want to be washed in the blood of Jesus and cleansed from all unrighteousness. All my needs are met because I am connected to the Source. In Jesus' name I pray, amen.

#GoGetThemBlessings

Take a dip in a pool or soak in the tub, and imagine that you are a frog, soaking up the source and presence of God. He is all around you.

WITHOUT CEASING

I love to work out. It's a consistent part of my life that focuses me and motivates me. But even if you aren't someone who hangs out in a gym, you're still training—in God's spiritual gym.

Believers who work out in God's spiritual gym are blessed. We aren't stumbling around, trying to find the best way to grow in wisdom or discern truth or increase our faith. We are being trained by a coach who trains only winners. God has already fought and won the battles we may encounter, and He is with us every step of the way to strengthen our muscles and turn us into elite champions for Him.

We may lose some rounds. We may stumble on occasion or face setbacks or unexpected challenges. But we learn from those individual losses. We focus. We build ourselves back up with the Holy Spirit's guidance. And in the end, God wins . . . and we win in His power.

Amid setbacks and hardship, keep seeking the proper training by saying, "God, I have faith. Help me in this battle." And when you're making gains, when you're seeing the fruit of the Spirit in your life, when God is opening doors and revealing His will, don't take your eyes off Him! Let your prayer conversation with God be as natural and consistent as the breaths you take. He is your coach in every moment, in every opportunity, in every need.

The Lord cannot lie. When He says He will help you and that if you ask it will be given to you, *it will happen.* I am a full testimony of that! I know the things I asked for and the things

I prayed about, and God has manifested them right before my eyes. But I had to have faith—even when it seemed like what I prayed for wasn't going to happen in the natural. He will do the same for you!

#LevelUpYourFaith

Lord, I come to you in prayer when times are rough, and I will continue to pray when times are great! I will pray when my eyes are filled with tears and when my eyes are brimming with joy. I will never stop praying no matter how I feel! And I thank You for never leaving my side. In Jesus' name, amen.

#GoGetThemBlessings

On social media this week, try to post daily about something you prayed about. Hashtag it #praywithoutceasing. What you share doesn't have to be detailed, but it will get you in a habit of stopping to pray with purpose, and it might inspire someone else to quiet their heart and go to God as well.

VICTORY

Arise, L<small>ORD</small>!
Deliver me, my God!
Strike all my enemies on the jaw;
break the teeth of the wicked.
PSALM 3:7

#BlessedMode

MMA is a crazy sport. Things get brutal! Bloody noses are split in half, teeth are broken, and faces are smashed up. I'm not lookin' to get in one of those rings!

In the spiritual realm, though, it's that same type of ferocious match. It's do or die because it's a war for our souls! And Satan will fight dirty. But you have something Satan will never have—God on your side. As long as you are in God's corner and on the right side of faith, you will win each round. That doesn't mean the fight will be easy or that you won't get a little banged up along the way, but God promises victory when we fight alongside him.

The Bible says a lot about this kind of heavenly battle:

- "The wages of sin is death; but the gift of God is eternal life through Jesus Christ our Lord" (Romans 6:23 KJV).
- "For our struggle is not against flesh and blood, but against the rulers, against the authorities, against the powers of this dark world and against the spiritual forces of evil in the heavenly realms" (Ephesians 6:12).
- "Submit yourselves, then, to God. Resist the devil, and he will flee from you" (James 4:7).

The Lord won't allow the Enemy to win (He has already defeated Satan!), but that doesn't mean we can just sit back. Satan still prowls about and will try to tear us away from God and His ways.

But guess what? *God just keeps blessing us*—even when life isn't going how we might hope. In the middle of whatever your struggle is, God continues to have the ultimate power. He keeps destroying the Enemy's plans. So what do we need to do? Stay close to God. Resist evil. Fight the battles we encounter. Notice the blessings. Thank God for His mercies. And watch for the victory that will come.

#LevelUpYourFaith

Lord, nothing is too big for You. I will never doubt You, only trust. You are victorious. In Jesus' name I pray, amen.

#GoGetThemBlessings

Download and play the song "Victory Is Mine" by Dorothy Norwood. It will bless you so much. The words are easy to memorize, and it is an awesome praise song about having the victory because you asked Jesus for help—and knowing that the devil is going to lose the battle.

90

He heals the brokenhearted and binds up their wounds.
PSALM 147:3

WOUNDS HEAL

#BlessedMode

Your body is made to heal. When you get hurt, it goes to work quickly, healing and closing up the wound. But it can still leave a scar that tells a story. When you get hurt, what do you do to help heal the wound? Apply an ointment so that it heals more quickly and avoids infection, and maybe scars less? I have a funny scar that always reminds me of the time I wanted to learn how to break-dance. I kept spinning on my elbow, and it gave me a nasty rug burn that left a permanent scar. But it reminds me that I got better at break dancing!

What about emotional wounds and scars—such as being hurt by a loved one, being abused, being lied to, or getting your heart broken? These take a different type of healing and leave a different type of scar. Our body does not immediately go into recovery mode for emotional wounds. They can take a long time to heal, and they are easier to hide because they're on the inside.

People everywhere walk around hurting on the inside. And you know the saying: "hurt people hurt people." Unforgiveness and bitterness are like infections. They can grow and rage out of control if they aren't treated. I know it's hard, but you must forgive yourself and others. The Lord will help you work through the pain. He can heal even the deepest wound and leave a beautiful scar in its place.

We must first recognize the hurt, and then allow the Lord to heal us. When you do this, the scar becomes a reminder and a testimony of what God has done in your life, how you have been changed and healed by God. And when people see your life and hear your story, they realize that God can heal them too.

Healing comes from the Lord! Ask Him now to step into your emotional wounds and start the healing process.

#LevelUpYourFaith

Lord, when I cried to You for help, You healed me. You delivered me from destruction. I listened closely and studied Your Word, and You gave me new life! Thank You so much. In Jesus' name I pray, amen.

#GoGetThemBlessings

Meditate on the words of today's Bible verse, and make the verse the lock screen on your phone. You'll see it every time you pick up your phone and be reminded of God's nearness.

BLESSED MONEY SEEDS

LEVEL UP
YOUR FAITH

Yes! You've finished this ninety-day devotional! I'm so happy for you! You rock! I hope you've grown closer to God and leveled up your faith. And I pray that you stay in blessed mode for the rest of your life.

I wrote this book to motivate believers to keep spreading the Good News, to stay strong in their faith, and to never give up on their dreams. I also wrote it to show how beautiful Jesus' love is and how He can change your life. As you read this book, if you found yourself wanting a closer relationship with Jesus, I have one more "go get 'em" for you to do—say the salvation prayer below.

This prayer of salvation means an eternity in heaven and a life on earth filled with joy, blessings, and goodness. Jesus gave us this gift when He died for us on the cross. But first I want to talk about why this prayer is important.

Why did Jesus come? He came to seek and to save the lost; to render powerless the devil's works over those who receive Jesus; and to provide healing to those oppressed by the devil. Why was mankind lost? God created Adam morally inno-cent, having a free will (the freedom of choice). God provided a situation for him to experience that choice. Adam's transgression brought spiritual death (alienation and separation from the life and nature of God) upon all men (Romans 5:12).

What is the solution to man's dilemma? The solution to man's state or dilemma is Jesus! "For God so loved the world, that he gave his only begotten Son, that whosoever believeth in him should not perish, but have everlasting life" (John 3:16 KJV).

How does one apply the solution? The application to the solution is a two-fold principle: confessing and believing. "If you acknowledge and confess with your mouth that Jesus is Lord [recognizing His power, authority, and majesty as God], and believe in your heart that God raised Him from the dead, you will be saved. For with the heart a person believes [in Christ as Savior] resulting in his justification [that is, being made righteous—being freed of the guilt of sin and made acceptable to God]; and with the mouth he acknowledges and confesses [his faith openly], resulting in and confirming [his] salvation" (Romans 10:9–10 AMP).

Is healing for all? Acts 10:38 states that Jesus went about doing good and healing all who were oppressed, for God was with Him. Healing is a part of our redemptive covenant: "That it might be fulfilled which was spoken by [Isaiah] the prophet, saying, Himself took our infirmities and bare our sicknesses" (Matthew 8:17 KJV).

Is salvation earned by doing good deeds, keeping the law, or by grace? Salvation is a free gift! "For by grace are ye saved through faith; and that not of yourselves: it is the gift of God: Not of works, lest any man should boast" (Ephesians 2:8–9 KJV).

Who are the children of God? You are not automatically a child of God simply because you grew up in church or you were confirmed. You must be adopted into the family of God by a new birth process. The scripture states, "But as many as received him, to them gave he power to become the sons of God, even to them that believe on his name" (John 1:12 KJV).

Now you understand why this is so important and why it's a celebration. This is the true divine access to Blessed Mode. Let's do this!

Dear God in heaven,

I come to You in the name of Jesus. Your Word says, "If you confess with your mouth the Lord Jesus and believe in your heart that God has raised Him from the dead, you will be saved. For with the heart one believes unto righteousness, and with the mouth confession is made unto salvation" (Romans 10:9–10 NKJV). I believe in my heart Jesus Christ is the Son of God. I believe He was raised from the dead for my justification, and I confess Him now as my Lord. I have now become the righteousness of God in Christ. I want to

thank You for taking spiritual torment for my sins, mental
distress for my worries and anxieties, and physical pain for
my sicknesses and diseases. By Your stripes I am healed, and
I receive salvation right now in Jesus' name. Amen.

Awesome! You did it! I am so happy for you! Blessed mode!

First, I want to give all honor and praise to God for making this book a reality. Thank You, Lord! It's going to bless so many people. Thank You for lighting my path and giving me the daily strength I need to get things done. Not my will, but Your will be done!

Writing my first book took a ton of focus and was strenuous at times, but it was also so rewarding and worthwhile, and it would not have been possible without the help of my beautiful, amazing wife, Asia. From hearing my ideas, helping me schedule out my days so I could have time to work on the book, to watching our loving and energetic children while I wrote in my office, to helping me pick out the cover art and giving me pep talks when needed . . . you are my everyday blessing, my gift from God, my best friend and prayer warrior. Thank you, my love! I love you so much and with all my heart, Asia!

Pastor Garry D. Zeigler and First Lady Antonia Zeigler, thank you for your guidance, your talks with me and Asia, and your prayers of protection over our family. The wisdom and knowledge you have given me over the years has been amazing. This book has been fueled by the guidance I got from you both while working in

Helps ministry and now working as a youth pastor at Spirit Food Christian Center. Thank you so much for being great mentors and spiritual teachers.

To my Spirit Food Christian Center family, thank you! Big shout-out to Minister Mebane for your prayers and for always keeping it real! Derek and Sophia Luke, thank you for being a big bro and sis to me and Asia and for giving advice and always sharing what the Lord puts on your heart. Thank you to Minister Anisha Bowman for having my back and covering Bible study for me when I had deadlines. Thank you, Erica Goings, for assisting and helping me while I minister to the teens on Sundays. And speaking of my amazing Spirit Food Teens, it is awesome seeing you all grow spiritually and become teens on fire for God! I'm enjoying being your youth pastor.

Thank you to my neighborhood church that I grew up in, to the leaders, teachers, and evangelists at Upright Missionary Baptist Church. The principles, songs, and Bible verses I learned at such a young age stayed with me all these years. Thank you, Rev. Milton Coleman Jr.

Huge thank you to Ruth Brown for teaching me how to fast and pray and destroy the works of the Enemy! Life got crazy for me in Los Angeles, and you helped me get spiritually connected to God. I enjoyed our prayer time so much. You were a big part of helping me mature in the Holy Spirit by showing me how to fight in the spiritual realm. My wife and I miss your prayers and singing, but we know you are with our heavenly Father.

Mom and Dad, thank you for telling everyone to "buy our son's new book!" I know you're going to do that, so I'm just saying thank you in advance. You both rock! I thank you both for showing me how important it is to keep learning and growing mentally and spiritually. It's always been a blessing seeing you both excited about new tasks, expanding your minds and taking on new adventures. I appreciate the love and support you give me and my siblings. Kenyatta and Kyra, thank you for the fun phone calls and group chats from Chicago during quarantine. Kyra and Hafiz, thank you for editing and uploading sermons on my YouTube while I focused on the finishing touches of the book.

Big hugs and thanks to my four children for making me a blessed and proud father! Wisdom, Honor, Allure, and Lyric, I hope this book will inspire you. Continue to dream big and trust in God, grabbing blessings while keeping God in your heart. Daddy loves you all.

Thank you to my agent, Brandi Bowles, who kept saying "Kel, you need to do a book." Thank you for the push! This has been an awesome experience. Thank you to my entire UTA team and to my management team at Levity Live. Alex, we did it! I appreciate you so much. Thank you, Mark Temple, for being the best entertainment lawyer.

Thank you to the HarperCollins team. You all are awesome! Thanks, Danielle Peterson, for your enthusiasm on every Zoom meeting. You made this entire process amazing! And my editors, Jennifer Gott and Bonnie Honeycutt, thank you both for your guidance!

I leave you all with this a quote from my grandfather-pastor, Elder Isaiah Heard Sr., who is looking down, smiling on us from heaven. He used to say, "May God bless you all real, real good."

I never understood why he put two "reals" in that sentence, but it felt good to hear it all the time. It was like Grandad was saying God is going to double the blessings! Thank you, Grandaddy, and give Grandma Sally a big hug for me!

Thank you all. Now go get them blessings.

Kel Mitchell is a world-renowned, two-time Emmy Award–nominated actor, writer, producer, and director. He has a deep acting resume that even includes finishing as runner-up in *Dancing With the Stars* in 2019. But he is best known for his roles in *Kenan & Kel*, *All That* and *Good Burger*. Most recently, he was a panelist on MTV's *Deliciousness* and is executive producer of the new *All That* reboot on Nickelodeon. Additionally, Kel is the host of the heartwarming TV series *Best Friends FurEver,* which airs Saturday mornings on CBS. He also recently starred as Double G, an impulsive and unpredictable billionaire rapper on *Game Shakers.*

When he is not acting, writing, or directing, Kel loves spending time with his family. He is really big on fitness and health, so he challenges himself with new and fun workouts. He also speaks to youth across the country, encouraging them to trust in the Lord and follow their dreams. Kel has been faithfully involved in Helps Ministry for more than eight years, and he became the youth pastor of Spirit Food Christian Center after Pastor Zeigler saw God's calling on his life to reach and teach the youth. Furthermore, he and his wife, Asia Lee-Mitchell, were honored with an award from the Carson Black Chamber of Commerce for providing a safe program for kids to show off their creative talents in their dance variety live show, *The Back House Party*. Kel is a spokesperson for Black College Expo, which provides numerous scholarships for students throughout the year. He is also a humanitarian and works very closely with the global Christian humanitarian organization World Vision.

Keep in touch with Kel:

Website: www.Kelmitchell.com

Instagram: @iamkelmitchell

Facebook: iamkelmitchell

Twitter: @iamkelmitchell

Church: www.spiritfoodchristiancenter.com

BLESSED MODE

BLESSED MODE

BLESSED

LEVEL UP
YOUR FAITH